- How to overcome denial and decipher the handwriting on the wall before it's too late
- How to move on if you decide to move out

If you're a previously effective manager caught up in a takeover, you know that the draining of energy and resulting sense of powerlessness can be appalling. The discouragement easily leads to the sometimes incorrect perception that you have no control over whether or not you will survive at your present company. The aim of *Surviving the 10 Ordeals of the Takeover* is to give you back every ounce of power that the chaos has drained from you. As author Robert Bell says about this book, "The only ax it has to grind is the one that it hopes to put into the hands of you, the manager, to help you survive."

Photo: Douglas Kent Hall

Robert Bell, Ph.D., is currently an associate professor in the economics department of Brooklyn College, City University of New York. He was formerly head of the management department at Fordham University's Graduate School of Business. Bell is the author of *You Can Win at Office Politics* (Times Books) and two other business books, and he writes for several national publications, including *Venture, Modern Maturity,* and *The New York Times.* Bell was awarded his doctorate in cybernetics at Brunel University in England.

Surviving the 10 Ordeals of the Takeover

Also by the author:

You Can Win at Office Politics
Having It Your Way
Decisions, Decisions with John Coplans

Surviving the 10 Ordeals of the Takeover

Robert Bell, Ph.D.

American Management Association

This book is available at a special
discount when ordered in bulk quantities.
For information, contact Special Sales Department,
AMACOM, a division of American Management Association,
135 West 50th Street, New York, NY 10020.

Library of Congress Cataloging-in-Publication Data

Bell, Robert, 1942-
   Surviving the 10 ordeals of the takeover.

   Includes index.
   1. Success in business. 2. Office politics.
3. Consolidation and merger of corporations.
I. Title. II. Title: Surviving the ten ordeals
of the takeover.
HF5386.B374   1988   650.1   87-47843
ISBN 0-8144-5902-1

©1988 Robert Bell
All rights reserved.
Printed in the United States of America.

This publication may not be reproduced,
stored in a retrieval system,
or transmitted in whole or in part,
in any form or by any means, electronic,
mechanical, photocopying, recording, or otherwise,
without the prior written permission of AMACOM,
a division of American Management Association,
135 West 50th Street, New York, NY 10020.

Printing number

10 9 8 7 6 5 4 3 2 1

To all who keep slugging

CONTENTS

INTRODUCTION 1

THE FIRST ORDEAL — The Niagara of Rumors 13

THE SECOND ORDEAL — Who Are These Guys? 35

THE THIRD ORDEAL — The Anglo Saxons versus the Normans 49

THE FOURTH ORDEAL — Nothing Is Getting Done 69

THE FIFTH ORDEAL — The Scramble To Fit In 81

THE SIXTH ORDEAL — The Tough Sell 99

THE SEVENTH ORDEAL — The Backstabbers 111

THE EIGHTH ORDEAL — The Handwriting on the Wall 123

THE NINTH ORDEAL — The Breakdown of Loyalty 139

THE TENTH ORDEAL — The Door 155

NOTES 171

INDEX 181

ACKNOWLEDGMENTS

Many people gave me encouragement and advice on this book. Quite a few of them are quoted herein, but others aren't. Although I would like to acknowledge the kindness of all of them, there really are too many to list. However, in particular I'd like to acknowledge Tom Fuchs, Douglas Kent Hall, Jeff Hodges, James Keogh, Ed Lutz, C. George Mates, Helen McEachrane, Philip R. O'Connell, Michael Pantaleoni, Barry Pascal, Paul Pavel, Michael Podgursky, Rosemarie Rochelle, Hy Sardy, and Ed Wilson.

A special thanks to Jonathan Dolger, my literary agent, and to Nancy Brandwein, my editor at AMACOM, for all their help.

Surviving the 10 Ordeals of the Takeover

INTRODUCTION

The middle managers were ready for their power breakfast. Assembled at a midtown Manhattan hotel at 7:30 A.M., they were all set for the formal announcement of the new direction their freshly restructured, multinational financial services company was about to take. Getting this kind of special attention, and having survived a series of layoffs, they were certain they had been tapped by top management as critical to its success.

And they were right; the company would not go forward in its new direction without firing them that morning. They were told not to go to their offices and never to turn up at the company again. Their severance checks were in the mail.

A true story? Yes. A brutal one? Sure. An exception? Only in its callousness. Mass firings of managers due to takeovers or restructuring have become daily events lately. Owners and top management have turned on the people who had been most supportive of them. As one headhunter said, "This system is eating itself alive."

This book is about and for the middle and upper managers caught up in these cataclysmic changes. Its focus is on you, the manager, and what you can and cannot expect and should and should not do at each point in the unfolding trauma. It is neither an apology for mergers nor a polemic against them. It is not an attack on top managers, nor is it an attempt to butter them up. It gives top management's side of things, insofar as there is one, because you must know it to survive. But it shows the hypocrisy in top management's position as well, because you must also know that to survive. This book is about realism. The only ax it has to grind is the one that it hopes to put into your hands, to help you survive.

How Many More Takeovers?

Although the Supreme Court recently gave the states the power to curb hostile takeovers, there is no major evidence that the ax is about to be hung back on the wall. Nor is it clear, as of this writing, that federal laws will be passed to put a brake on them. Both Congressman John Dingell, the powerful chairman of the House Energy and Commerce Committee and Senator William Proxmire, head of the Senate Banking Committee, have introduced bills on the matter. Both bills are strongly opposed by the Reagan Administration, and neither appears certain of passage. In fact, the stockmarket crash on Monday, October 19, 1987, may have been provoked in part by action of the House Ways and Means Committee on a bill that would restrict interest deductions on junk bonds used in takeovers. Speculators may have dumped their stock, contributing to the crash. A little over a week after the crash, the Chairman of the Committee, Congressman Dan Rostenkowski, said he was willing to reconsider the interest issue. In any case, the crash created new takeover opportunities by cutting the stock price of potential targets, thereby making them cheaper to takeover.

Even an earlier change in the federal tax laws, which was expected to slow down the merger mania, has not done it as of this writing, five months after the new law went into effect. In fact, merger activity in 1987 showed a $28 billion increase over the same period one year earlier, when the old tax laws held sway.

The previous three years had been banner ones for takeovers, mergers, divestitures, and leveraged buyouts. There were 3,001 of these deals in 1985, setting a 12-year record and edging out 1984's total, which itself was a 10-year record. In 1986 even more deals were struck—3,336 of them. But the dollar total of $179.8 billion was bigger in '85, than in '86, which had a mere $173.1 billion. This is because '86 had only 26 deals worth a billion dollars or more, while '85 had 36 of them. Either year was good news for deal makers, who continued to pop the corks off champagne bottles in celebration.

Introduction

But the top and middle level executives manning the companies being traded have had anything but a corking good time. For them, these years have been among the most stressful in American business history.

How Many Managers Have Been Hit So Far?

Nobody seems to know the answer to this question. Outplacement consultants, who counsel fired managers on how to get another job, nearly always emphasize that staff jobs are hit hardest. They point out that when two companies merge there is usually only room for one corporate PR executive, and one corporate planning chief, and one corporate financial officer, and so forth. The experience of being the wrong staff people happened to executives at Continental International when it was taken over by Peter Kiewit Sons, an Omaha construction company. Virtually all of Continental's 300 corporate staff members were let go.

According to a study by Lamalie Associates, executive recruiters, covering the years 1982 through 1984, almost half the 150 executives in the biggest takeover targets got out within a year. Most left because they didn't like the way their new bosses did things. Only one-fifth said their jobs had been scrapped. CEOs of companies taken over had about the same experience, according to Hayes/Hill, a Chicago management consulting firm. Its study of 200 CEOs who were at the receiving end of the takeover showed that 43 percent hit the road before two years had passed.

But far more than staff executives get the ax as a consequence of mergers and restructurings. Line people get "displaced" too. That's the Bureau of Labor Statistics' euphemism for people whose jobs vaporize after plant closings. Their jobs simply vanish, as if zapped by Darth Vader. Most of these people, of course, are blue-collar workers. But a lot are managers, some of them in service industries. For example, when Wells Fargo gobbled up Crocker National Bank in May of 1986, it fired 1,600 managers the day the deal closed. None of Crocker's top brass was spared.

A 1984 Bureau of Labor Statistics survey of 703,000 displaced managers and professionals looked into the issue. The survey considered managers and professionals who had worked for at least three years in one job and lost it or left it between January 1979 and January 1984 as a result of abolition of the job, slack work, plant closings, or relocations. By far, most of the displaced went back to work again. Only about 17 percent were unemployed at the end of the survey, and almost 9 percent had dropped out of the labor force, in most cases presumably taking early retirement. The remaining 75 percent were holding down new jobs. Looked at this way, things don't seem so bad.

But the same study showed that their new jobs weren't always so hot. Of 342,000 who were back at a desk, a little over one-fourth had taken a pay cut of at least 20 percent. Another 13 percent had also been squeezed in the paycheck, but by no more than 20 percent. However, some made out fine. Just over 30 percent said their new jobs paid more than 20 percent above their old jobs. Another 30 percent were up, but less than 20 percent from their old jobs. This was only one study, although a huge one. Another study, by the U.S. Labor Department's Bureau of International Labor Affairs, showed a 16 percent average drop in pay for managers. The bottom line? Nobody knows for sure, but it's obvious that things don't necessarily work out for the best when managers get pushed out the door.

Of those managers and professionals who rebounded, how long had they been on their backsides? The government studies aren't specific on this since they do not break out managers from their fellow blue-collar victims. But for the whole 5.1 million workers displaced between 1979 and 1984, 2.2 million, or 43 percent, were without jobs for at least 27 weeks of the 5-year period.

Fortune magazine recently looked at this same question, conducting its own survey of 250 executives who were looking for work. The magazine knew they were looking because they had sent their resumés to an executive search firm, E. A. Butler and Associates, during the first six months of 1986. The results weren't vastly different from those of the government's survey. Of these displacees, 4 percent had an exceedingly rough time, taking between 13 and 23 months to get another job. Another 9 percent took between 10 months and a year to get hired. And an additional 23 percent took 7 to 9 months. Adding these percentages up gives 36 percent who were job hunting for at least 28 weeks. Add to this the biggest single category, 43 percent, who took 4 to 6 months, and it becomes apparent that it's hard for most executives to get a new job. Only 21 percent found new jobs within 3 months.

The *Fortune* survey is especially helpful in that it includes executives who still had jobs but were looking to change. This would include people who had heard rumors of corporate doom and got on the stick before the maniac with the ax arrived.

Are Jobs Being Destroyed in Vain?

This is another question for which there is no definitive answer. One group, some of whom are making a fast buck off the mergers and restructuring, insist the whole thing is enhancing the competitiveness of industry. But another group, some of whom are making money from the pretakeover set-up, say the mergers are making industry less competitive and in fact are turning the U.S. economy into one of extractive industries and hamburger stands.

Typical of the comments of the pro-takeover crowd who are not themselves making millions on the raids are those of Professor Michael C. Jenson, of both the Graduate School of Management, University of Rochester, and the Harvard Business School. Words from a double-barreled professor should not be dismissed out of hand. He testified before a 1985 House Subcommittee chaired by then-Congressman Tim Worth:

> This restructuring of corporate America I believe is healthy and should not be restricted. Divestitures, split-ups, and liquidations, are an important part of this activity that is breathing new life into corporate America, shaking up the old ways of doing things and generating large benefits.
>
> Divestitures and liquidations do not mean the assets are thrown away or dumped on the scrap heap, but rather that the assets are redeployed to more valuable and productive uses....

More testimony along the same lines was provided at the same House hearing by Joseph R. Wright, Jr., deputy director of the Office of Management and Budget:

> Takeovers ... often take place because a company's management, for any one of a number of reasons, has over a long period failed to deliver to stockholders the full value of the assets owned by that company. In such cases, takeover bids provide stockholders with the chance to realize the value incumbent management has been unable to deliver.

This is a restatement of the classic economics argument made in an academic article by Henry G. Manne over 20 years ago: "Only the takeover scheme provides some assurance of competitive efficiency among corporate managers and thereby affords strong protection to the interests of . . . non-controlling stockholders."

Raider T. Boone Pickens also testified at the 1985 House hearing. Here's what a man who has been showered with staggering wealth from mergers has to say on the matter:

> Do not be misled by the notion that merger activity in the threat of a takeover diverts management away from its duties. If management had been fulfilling those duties and keeping the share price up, it would not be vulnerable to takeover. Mergers do not divert management from managing. It diverts them from fishing and hunting camps.

The mergermen argue that there are macroeconomic data showing the benefit of takeovers both for the companies involved and for the entire economy. They base their arguments on an economic model advocated at the University of Chicago. They have produced studies showing that the stock market price of the taken-over company goes up in the four weeks just before it gets swallowed. The stock price of the buying company, in these studies, usually stays the same, or in some studies rises a little bit. This is alleged to show that value has been created, the market realizing that the combined company will be more efficient than the separate pieces. With this happening all over the economy, the efficiency of the entire economy is alleged to increase as well.

Not everyone buys this definition of creating value. A prominent antihostile-takeover lawyer, Leigh B. Trevor, has said, "They say hostile takeovers create wealth, and in order to establish that principle they cite the surprising proposition that stock prices go up when a premium bid is made. That, I think, equally supports the proposition that I'd be glad to sell my house for twice what it's worth." In other words, the announcement of a takeover bid simply signals that a stock may jump in price, and the bandwagon gets moving as people find cash from any source and dump it into stock certificates.

But the mergermen aren't the only ones with stock price studies. The antimergermen have shown that if the stock price analysis is extended for a couple of years after the merger, by which time the alleged efficiencies should really get rolling, the stock price of the buying company actually falls to the level of those of companies in businesses of the same risk level that did not merge. These studies also point out that even if the stock price goes up and stays there, the

Introduction

increase could be due simply to tax advantages, not to increased efficiencies.

If there are no indisputable, hard macroeconomic *data* in support of mergers, there is no shortage of anecdotes of fat, flabby, sloppy companies becoming lean, mean, muscular ones as a result of mergers. This is the Jack LaLanne theory of business economics. *Fortune* ran down a list of several companies that, it said, got leaner and meaner. It described what it said were successes at Monsanto and the spun-off parts of Continental Group, with Kiewit retaining only the original Continental Can Company. This, according to the article, had been treated as a cash cow and overmilked. Donald L. Sturm, Kiewit's vice chairman, is quoted as saying, "Continental Group ended up starving the golden goose. We had to refeed it."

Other companies discussed in the *Fortune* article were Unicol and Phillips Petroleum, which, according to the article, "later succeeded in fighting Pickens off only at the price of adopting much of his economically efficient program." The article went on to state that $8.7 billion had been "returned" to shareholders, and that the two oil companies dropped their "grandiose expansion ambitions" to cover the huge debt they assumed to make shareholders want to sell to them rather than to Pickens.

Although interviews for this book tended to confirm the analysis of the consequences of the Continental Group takeover, those for Phillips, which fought off both Pickens and Icahn, did not.

Phillips, which bought back half its stock, had a debt of $8.6 billion by April 1985. It sold assets worth $2 billion, bringing its equity down to $5.9 billion. It ended up with a debt-to-equity ratio of 80 percent, cutting its capital budget by 30 percent, almost entirely from exploration and production. Moody's, concerned that the cut in capital spending could deplete reserves and destroy the company, reduced its debt ratings on $6.1 billion of Phillips's long-term debt. Nor did Phillips's high debt put the company in great shape when oil prices dropped from over $28 per barrel to $12 to $15 per barrel.

Nearly two years before *Fortune* presented its anecdotes, *Business Week* laid out its own episodic tales after noting that "the overall record of companies merged in recent years is not encouraging. One out of three acquisitions is later undone." The article then went on to list several takeovers and mergers that have "gone sour," including Flour and St. Joe ("incompatible corporate cultures"); Mobil and Marcor ("overpaid for unfamiliar business"); and Wickes and Gamble-Skogmo ("no strategic fit").

As we'll see in later chapters, there is even harder evidence that mergers may be a bad idea more often than not, but for the moment, we don't need to jump to that conclusion. What we know for sure is that the anecdotal evidence is inconclusive.

There may be some macroeconomic data that mergers aren't necessarily such a hot idea. However, the data are not from the current wave of mergers, but from the go-go years of the sixties and early seventies, when many of the conglomerates currently getting dismembered were put together. Economist F. M. Scherer, of Swarthmore College and the Brookings Institution, looked not at stock price, but at profitability. He surveyed the studies on the matter and found that on average, the gobbled-up companies weren't the lousy performers, but were as profitable as those that weren't eaten alive. This suggests that the taken-over management was at least no worse than the rest of the crowd. Keep in mind that this is *on average*. Some of the displaced managers undoubtedly were turkeys. But since this is an average, some must have been better than most too.

Examining specific business lines after the mergers, Scherer determined that these lines tended to be slightly *less* profitable after the mergers. And this was true whether the merger had been hostile, "White-Knighted," or without management screaming. Less profitable? If mergers are so efficient, these business lines are supposed to be more profitable! What happened? Scherer's research kicked the mergermen right in their junk bonds:

> ... most of the observed post-takeover performance deficiency was associated with the higher asset values and depreciation charges that result from the payment of substantial premiums over pre-merger book value to effectuate the takeover. Once those revaluation effects are factored out, there is no evidence that the acquiring companies managed their acquired assets either clearly worse or clearly better than the average of the industries to which the acquired lines belonged.

So much for the mergermen either seeing how to increase efficiency or being able to do much more about it than anyone else.

Anti-hostile-takeover lawyer Leigh Trevor has an explanation for this:

> What you in fact see in the real world, I believe, is that the threat of hostile takeovers focuses management attention on short-term planning.... That threat emphasizes performance measured by earnings per share improvements from quarter to quarter. That threat also diverts a

Introduction

great deal of time and money to defensive planning to deal with the hostile takeover. . . .

Beyond this, those who don't like hostile takeovers point at the staggering flight from equity, $90 billion in 1984 alone, and the even more staggering increase in debt. "Both successful takeover moves and all of the defensive tactics, greenmail, what we are now calling 'restructuring,' the leveraged buyout phenomenon, all do the same thing: extract equity from the corporation and replace it with debt. Either way, the company loses," testified Andrew C. Sigler to Congressman Wirth's Subcommittee. Sigler is the CEO of Champion International and Chairman of the Business Roundtable's Corporate Responsibility Task Force.

For example, to fight off takeovers, CBS, Phillips, Union Carbide, Unocal, and Atlantic Richfield borrowed in total $33.5 billion. With all this debt being run up, we shouldn't be surprised that corporate debt is dropping in quality. In 1985, Standard & Poor downgraded the debt of 265 companies and upgraded that of only 125.

These are only some of the issues involved in an overview of merger mania. Opponents of mergers usually point to other issues as well: One is the devastating effect on local communities. We'll look at several examples in this book. Another is the enormous opportunity costs these mergers involve. All that money sunk into paying off junk bonds could be spent on something useful, such as research and development. Instead, so the argument goes, tomorrow is traded for yesterday. For example, in 1985, "spending on mergers exceeded combined expenditures for R&D and net new investment," according to two prominent economists writing in *The New York Times*. The third objection might be called the parasite effect. It focuses on the colossal bundles pocketed by the deal-making lawyers, investment bankers, and corporate officers with their golden parachutes. For example, when Pantry Pride bought Revlon, the deal price was $1.8 billion and the transactions costs were $226 million—more than 10 percent of the deal price. In 1986, "an estimated $1.2 billion was sucked from" the living, dying, and dead corporations involved in mergers, according to David Weber, writing in *California Business*.

Mergers also tend to get a bad press, sometimes for good reason. The deaths of Corky and Orky illustrate this. They were two trained whales in Marineland, California. An entire generation of kids who had visited the place had grown up loving these creatures who would jump up from the tank and kiss their trainers. Then publisher Harcourt Brace Jovanovich bought the place. It said the tank was bad and moved the two whales out in the middle of the night. But the movers did something dreadfully wrong, because the two beloved whales suffered horrible deaths in transit. Then the new owners put the Marineland property up for sale. The public outcry was deafening, with Peter Jovanovich, the executive VP and son of the CEO, running around trying to explain. "This is the worst public relations thing since [the company began publishing books] in 1919," he told *Los Angeles Times* reporter Tim Waters.

The Ten Ordeals

Managers in nearly every company that goes through one of these turning points suffer through roughly the same sorts of protracted torture, which this book calls *ordeals*. Some of these ordeals, such as the Niagara Falls of rumors and the breakdown in loyalty, have been widely reported. Others, such as flip-flopping in your mind on whether or not you can fit into the new structure or facing the fact that the handwriting on the wall spells out your name, have not been so widely discussed but are instantly recognizable to people who have suffered through them.

For previously effective managers caught up in one of these traumas, the draining of energy and resulting sense of powerlessness left by these ordeals can be appalling. The discouragement can easily lead to a sometimes incorrect perception—that you have no control over whether or not you will survive at your company.

The aim of this book is to give you back every ounce of power the chaos has drained from you. The way this will be accomplished is by separately focusing on each of these ordeals in order to steel you for them. This book separates the takeover chaos into ten distinct ordeals. But the number isn't magic; other approaches could analyze a few more or a few less. The key is to look at each one to understand why it is there and how you can understand it sufficiently to get past it. The goal is not to wallow in the suffering, but to overcome it, so you can leave it behind you.

The book shows you what you can do to survive at your present company in the event of a takeover. It does not offer a panacea—there is no way to guarantee hanging onto your job. In fact, depending on the circumstances, this isn't always desirable for an effective manager. But the book looks into all the angles for determining whether or not you should stay, and if so, how to do it.

Following is a brief rundown on the Ten Ordeals.

Introduction

The First Ordeal: The Niagara of Rumors. Should you ignore the rumors? Join in? Start your own? How do you separate the truth out of them? Are the official pronouncements and unofficial encouragements of top management any more truthful? Less truthful? We'll look at actual events to get at the best way to deal with these and other issues.

The Second Ordeal: Who Are These Guys? How do you find out about your new bosses before it's too late? Should you try to find out? So often these people don't know what they're doing, how come? We'll reap the insights of a variety of consultants who advise on these matters and executives who have been through the mill. Forewarned *is* forearmed in this case.

The Third Ordeal: The Anglo Saxons versus the Normans. Why are these new bosses so arrogant? Why is there so much resentment toward them? How can you avoid the resentment without losing the cooperation of those who have some control over your future? Does it make any difference whether the new owner is a corporate raider or an Establishment corporation represented on the Roundtable? Actual cases will illustrate the issues here and answer the key questions.

The Fourth Ordeal: The Scramble to Fit In. This is the most sinister of the ordeals because it strikes at your self-confidence. We'll look at the critical questions top management will be asking itself *about* you even if it doesn't dare ask these questions *to* you. We'll also look at the key questions you should ask yourself. Actual experiences of people who went through this ordeal will illustrate the answers.

The Fifth Ordeal: Nothing Is Getting Done. Work may have come to a screeching halt, but you need to shine in order to increase your chances of being picked for survival or even promotion. How do you do it? What are the strategies of people who have succeeded in these situations? How do you get the people who work under you to keep at it? A number of people who have remained effective and promotable during this stage of the takeover will tell their stories.

The Sixth Ordeal: The Big Sell. We'll show how you can take the initiative not only to sell your skills to the new owners but also to have key customers do some selling for you. Some of the advice on how to sell yourself is disputed by different people who have prospered in takeovers, and we'll look at both sides of the issue. We'll also look at how to handle one of the most traumatic events in selling yourself—the retention interview.

The Seventh Ordeal: The Backstabbers. Although some people disagree over the extent of backstabbing by people you had previously counted on in takeovers, there is no doubt that it does happen, and there are certain ploys to guard against—the poison umbrella, log-rolling deals, and going by the book to slice up whole departments are examples. These and others will be discussed and illustrated with actual cases.

The Eighth Ordeal: The Handwriting on the Wall. To see the handwriting you have to overcome denial, the belief that nothing drastically bad will happen to you. The chapter will show the catastrophic consequences of failing to overcome denial and give some pointers on how you can overcome it. Once you can see it, what are the signs to look for? The chapter will help you to decipher them. A wide range of graffiti will be looked at, including such widely diverse wall scrawlings as people suddenly craving your wisdom or becoming utterly indifferent to you. The special graffiti that shows up at retention interviews will also be pointed out.

The Ninth Ordeal: The Breakdown of Loyalty. This is one ordeal of the takeover that doesn't end. Everybody knows that loyalty has diminished, but by how much? Is it still a factor you have to consider if you move on to another company, or are you a sucker if you do? We'll look at the trends that are weakening loyalty to see whether they've played themselves out. Can you fake loyalty? Should you try? The chapter will provide some answers.

The Tenth Ordeal: The Door. If you haven't survived the other ordeals, you face the tenth one—when you're out of the corporation and trying to figure out what's next. Should you sue? How do you find a good lawyer? Is a good lawyer one who advises you to sue? Is outplacement a good idea? Are there alternatives if the company won't spring for it, or even if it will? Where are the new jobs and how much can you get? Is consulting really a viable option? The chapter will give some answers and illustrate them with case studies.

None of these ordeals will go away even if you understand and anticipate them. But why let them take you by surprise? The following chapters may help you to increase your chances of surviving these traumas. You'll see what to expect and what other people advise and have done when they went through these wringers.

1
THE FIRST ORDEAL
The Niagara of Rumors

"There were rumors—*hourly* rumors," said C. J. "Pete" Silas, CEO of Phillips Petroleum, in an interview about how he handled the runs on his company by Carl Icahn and T. Boone Pickens.

There was a great deal to rumor about. By the time the episodes had settled down, the staff at corporate headquarters in Bartlesville, Oklahoma, was slashed by about one-third, dropping from roughly 7,800 to around 5,000 as a result of layoffs and three separate early retirement programs. Rushing so many people out the door "feeds uncertainty" for those who have not yet gotten the bad news, said the chairman. The nightmare was worsened because the jobs were cut in a town of only 35,000 people. "You can't walk across the street anywhere and get a job," added Silas.

And all of this was the result of two *successful* fights against takeovers.

Once the word on an impending takeover gets out, the cascade of rumors is "the major thing that happens" inside executive offices, says Robert J. Lee, president of Lee-Hecht and Associates of New York, outplacement consultants. Champion International's CEO, Andrew Sigler, has been quoted in *The New York Times* as saying essentially the same thing: "People sit around and talk. That's all they do. They're scared to death," which is great for Robert L. Lee. He and other outplacement consultants are in a booming industry now as a result of the takeover and retrenchment frenzy.

For example, when Irwin Jacobs made a hostile but ultimately successful run on the diversified sports products and energy services company, AMF Inc., Drake, Beam and Morin, the world's largest outplacement consultants, got the business. The first layoffs, 150, in White Plains, New York, and Stamford, Connecticut, happened just before Jacobs's tender offer was announced. The company said it was decentralizing its operations. Immediately after the takeover, another 140 employees were cut, and corporate staff was down to fewer than 60 jobs. A few months later, in October, *all* of the corporate staff jobs in the area were abolished, although as many as ten people were asked to relocate to Minneapolis.

This was a multi-billion-dollar deal. But a similar fate meets managers at smaller outfits, for example, those at the Conwed Corporation of St. Paul, Minnesota. After a ten-week fight, the company was taken over by Cardiff Acquisitions, La Jolla, California, for $44 million. The acquirer is a subsidiary of Leucardia National Corporation, ten-percent owner of Irwin Jacobs's Minstar. Before the takeover, there were 1,600 employees. Afterwards, the total was 900. All 700 employees at a profitable plant in Cloquet, Minnesota, were terminated. Of these 700 people, 140 were offered the chance to relocate to other Conwed plants on the East Coast. Four hundred jobs at the Cloquet plant were retained, and the 560 remaining terminated people were allowed to apply for them. About 200 were rehired—at three dollars per hour less than before. Most of Conwed's corporate staff of 175 was dumped within a year of the takeover.

The same sort of thing happened at McQuay, Inc., a Plymouth, Massachusetts, manufacturer of air conditioners, heaters, radiators, and ice-making equipment bought for $30 million by a Dallas company, Snyder General Corporation. Before the takeover, there were 3,500 employees, afterwards, only 1,000. Eight of the twelve vice presidents who were there before the takeover were not there afterwards.

No wonder this sort of wholesale slaughter has been called the "Pol Pot method of doing takeovers" and the "killing field of corporate America" by one of its major opponents, Leigh Trevor, a Cleveland lawyer who defends the targets. This is the context, and these are the stories on the minds of managers when the first whisper of an impending takeover or retrenchment is heard.

But that's the last time a whisper will be heard; the roar of the rumors will soon drown it out.

The Rumors Before the Deal

"Rumors started to fly on who's going to buy. In our case, a lot of foreign companies were looking at the firm. This made us all more anxious—we couldn't second guess them and upper management would be locked up with foreigners."

That's what the 29-year-old head of the mergers, acquisitions, and divestitures department of a subsidiary of a major conglomerate said when he suddenly heard that *his* subsidiary had been put on the block.

But that wasn't all the initial rumors dealt with, added the displaced mergerman: "The other concern is how much they pay for the company. They can pay more because they can borrow cheaper. But the more they pay, the more they have to earn." And, this meant, the more staff jobs they might have to ax. Since he had formerly been a man who did the takeovers, the irony of his being on the wrong side of the money didn't escape him. "Now I'm not in control," he said, adding, "Someone else is out there with notebook in hand—it makes you stop and think about the lives that mergers and acquisitions affect."

All the rumors are fueled by operations on (or under) Wall Street. The rumors are also driven by essentially the same things that drive Wall Street itself—fear and greed. Fear for one's job and career, greed in that there just may be an opportunity lurking there. The first wave of rumors inevitably seems to be about the deal itself. People are trying to figure out what it is, so they can make some sense of what's in it for them. This, of course is perfectly rational. They would be fools not to do this. A perfect example was reported in *The Corporate Communications Report*. The director of investor relations for St. Joe Minerals Corporation, Kathleen Kucera, phoned an adviser to the company, a friend of hers. Seagram Company had just bid $45 cash per share for her company. "I said, 'Off the record, what do you think?'" she reported. "The company is gone," he replied.

Her friend was right, but not about Seagram's bid, which was topped by one from a "White Knight," Flour Corporation, which offered $60 per share. Kucera summed up her feelings on how to assess a deal once a company has been put on the block:

> I think that anyone knowledgeable about such situations knows that once the company is in play, the likelihood is probably 95% that it's gone. It's the rare company that

has somebody come after them, particularly with a cash offer, and isn't gone quite quickly.

The rumors of impending takeovers can start even when the company isn't "in play," or likely to be. For example, the Silicon Valley has been plagued with retrenchments and shutdowns in the mid-1980s. Twenty-five percent of the local and worldwide workforce of the nine biggest chip makers was laid off between January 1985 and January 1986. This has prompted rumors of impending takeovers. The rumors are obviously generated by fear, but there may be no valid basis for them, according to an article by Christopher Schmitt in the *San Jose Mercury News*. The article quoted Adam Cuhney, an analyst from the San Francisco branch of Kidder, Peabody: "There's no interest in buying semiconductor companies at all. . . . There's too much capacity."

What would it take to put some validity into the otherwise irrational rumors? Bargains. Cuhney pointed to the purchase by the French company, Thomson S.A., of Mostek, at 20 percent of book value. But this was an unusually low price.

So rumors can sometimes be blown away with a rational analysis. But one of the striking things about the torrent of rumors is that the motivation for them is rational. In the absence of hard data, everything and anything can be important.

The rumor roar, however, starts with neither a bang nor a whimper. The first sound people usually hear, just before any news leaks out regarding a possible takeover, is the sound of silence. A 30-year-old woman, an assistant VP at a New York real estate consulting company taken over by a huge investment bank, reported, "Basically, no one talked to anyone but their cliques. A silence developed which broke down team effort." She reported that executives who had previously hung around kibitzing suddenly and for no apparent reason lost their appetite for trading jokes and kidding around. She added, "In retrospect I realize that the *absence* of talk is the giveaway that something is up."

One reason for the absence of top executives from the usual small-talk gatherings is that they may be in meetings trying to figure out what is going on. A former top executive at the Continental Group told this story in an interview:

> The stock had jumped the day before, so there was an early morning, June 4th, meeting of the executives to figure out why. In the middle of it, the secretary came in. "I have a long distance call from Sir James Goldsmith," she said. Someone else said, "Get your resumé up to

date." Up to that point, there were no rumors. Everything had been fine.

The silence and the sudden absence of managers may be a very common phenomenon. Price Pritchett, a consultant on a number of mergers, has said,

> . . .people begin to play their cards much closer to their chest. The information channels receive less input that is dependable. And the data that is submitted is more likely to be filtered, distorted, or edited out completely before it reaches its intended destination.

It seems that virtually everyone has an increased appetite for information and a diminished willingness to feed honest, accurate data to others.

Invaluable Gossip

To understand the full significance of this, we have to appreciate the pivotal role played by the grapevine in large organizations. The pivotal role of the grapevine? Rumors? Gossip? They're important? You bet.

The idealized notion that people get most of their information from official channels doesn't meet the test of common experience. For example, did you get your job through an ad, a job posting, or, if an entry level job, a college recruiter? In other words, did you get your job through a publicly available source? Maybe. A lot of people have. But quite a few managers have done essentially what some of those who have lately been nailed for takeovers themselves have done—they've traded on inside information. A friend tipped them off that there was an opening, and they went for it.

More commonly, in the event of a takeover or merger, people find through the grapevine that they're about to lose their jobs. At the Silicon Valley microchip manufacturer Advanced Micro Devices, according to an article in the *San Jose Mercury News*, 500 people were suddenly laid off, including many managers. Typical of the experiences were those of one middle manager, who was making $48,000 per year. His boss gave him exactly 20 minutes to pack up and get out after he and others got the death news. However, the grapevine had helped this man the night before. A senior manager with a conscience and a sense of decency had tipped off the victim. "I had at least enough time to stay late Thursday night and get my resumé done and make up a list of contacts, my network," reported the man doing the packing. He added, "Thank God I had a very long list, based on the time I've been here."

But this didn't save him from an unpleasant scene. His boss stood over him with a checklist as the victim filled a cardboard box that had been left outside his office. "It was very humiliating to [have him] stand there, with his checklist, while I packed," reported the fired manager.

Incidentally, according to a survey by the U.S. General Accounting Office, 23 percent of white-collar layoffs and 24 percent of blue-collar ones occur with no notice at all.

So being attached to a grapevine has a couple of obvious advantages. It can get you into a job, and it can also get you out of one with a better chance of securing the next one. Over the past few years, women's groups, called *networks*, have organized specifically for the purpose of creating grapevines for private channels of information. In fact, outplacement consultants, hired by top management in a takeover to soften the blow on those they dump, train the dumped in how to create networks to get another job. The outplacement counselors are training the victims on how to grow grapevines.

The irony is that some of these people being trained in grapevine growing are themselves victims of illegal grapevines. Some were even victimized by the most notorious illegal grapevine of recent years, Ivan Boesky's.

Ivan Boesky said in his book, *Merger Mania*, "Risk arbitrage is not gambling in any sense. Done properly, the odds of a risk arbitrage investment are with you, not against you." What he *didn't* say in his book is that the "proper" way to shift the odds in one's favor is to cheat by creating an illegal grapevine. However, this became clear when he agreed to fork over $100 million to the federal government for his role in grapevining with people outside his own organization, including people in Wall Street brokerage houses such as Goldman Sachs and Kidder Peabody.

Of course, Boesky and his pals are the exception, right? Maybe not. A recent study by the Securities and Exchange Commission of 172 takeovers between 1981 and 1985 revealed an interesting fact. In every single case, the stock of the company ultimately acquired rose at least 26.5 percent during the three weeks before the takeover was announced. This was the minimum rise, which happened when there were no press reports, no widespread rumors, and no SEC filings of positions suddenly taken. If there *had been* such rumors or SEC filings, the stock price would have jumped around 50 percent. The report said it was "unable to explain a great deal of the pre-bid

The Niagara of Rumors

trading." Even the rumors might have started with illegal inside dope. The study said, "It is possible and logical to many, that illegal insider trading behavior could affect" the spread of rumors and press reports.

All of this is important to managers caught up in takeovers, not only because they could be victimized by these shenanigans, but also to counter a line endlessly put out by top management—that middle managers should not get involved in the "rumor mill." But the evidence here suggests that many in top management are enriching themselves through their own private rumor mills. Thus the admonition to stay away from the rumor mills should be taken in its full context.

This context was laid out in an article in *The New York Times* by Stephen A. Schwarzman, president of a private investment bank, the Blackstone Group:

> One difficulty has been the number of people who have prior knowledge of a deal. A buyout or acquisition may start in the office of a company's chief executive officer, but others in the company and many outsiders soon learn of it. The company's investment bankers review the transaction for potential conflicts of interest and for inclusion on a confidential—but not completely inaccessible—restricted list of stocks that the firm is barred from trading. Young analysts make inquiries of research services, while merger advisers sometimes talk to traders and arbitragers for an assessment of tactics.
>
> Soon, lawyers, accountants, and specialized consultants join the team. Committees at banks and financial intermediaries are approached for financing. And each strand of this widening web is accompanied by secretaries, messengers and printers.

Of course, this book is not recommending insider trading. But the techniques of grapevining both inside and outside one's company can be used to protect oneself from exploitation by those who do grapevine illegally. Specifically, grapevining can be used for employment purposes.

This is precisely what is recommended by many management consultants, who essentially urge managers to seek out the same kinds of information the insider crooks do even if they don't plan to use it for illegal purposes. They rarely put it this way, but this is what it comes down to. How do you network within the company? It's easy, according to John P. Sullivan of Management Campus in

Atlanta. "Take someone you don't know to lunch," he advises, adding, "Always have time for building relationships within the company."

But can you believe what you hear from these people whom you don't really know? "Managers tend to believe the rumors more than not," says independent consultant John Artise, 39, who has counseled fired executives at Kodak, NBC, AT&T, W. R. Grace, Phelps Dodge, Chase Manhattan Bank, and other firms:

> They believe the rumors come from someone close to the top who has leaked the information or from sources that are blatantly open—papers left in wastebaskets that were not completely shredded and then were seen by cleaning people, or from people who have had a little too much to drink at lunch and then let themselves run off at the mouth.

Should managers believe the cleaning people? Artise says yes. "The track record has already been established that if you get it from the cleaning people, it's probably true." But other consultants are skeptical. Sullivan, of Management Campus, said of this, "The janitors? How many can read?" However, he suggests that the principle might be sound even if the specific avenue isn't. As an alternative source of seemingly low level but potentially useful information, he suggests, without recommending it, that one could become friendly with the waiter at the hideaway restaurant where top people are known to go. Sullivan recalls that years before, when he was starting out in the corporate world, there had been a shoeshine stand in the office of his building, and this was the only stand in the area. All the top executives stopped there for a shine, and the shoeshine man heard quite a lot of inside information. "I got my shoes shined there regularly and became friendly with the guy," recalls Sullivan.

Befriending the cleaning people or the shoeshine man is simply an example of networking with people who provide services to the company. The floor scrubbers, of course, are at the bottom of the pecking order of those providing services. What about those closer to the top? Other possible sources of information you aren't supposed to know about are Big Eight accountants. Nearly all the Fortune 500 firms are audited by them. "They're the best source," says Artise, adding, "they're always there doing audits, so they're always interfacing with high-level managers—lunch, dinner, staying late, overnight trips. They hear stuff that has nothing to do with the audits." Many are young, lonely, and away from home. If they thought you were their friend, they might tell you something that would not breech the integrity of their audit but might save your career.

One group that has been documented as a source are former and possibly disgruntled senior managers of companies. An example of this occurred in 1987 when a group organized by Asher Edelman tried to take over Burlington Industries. A federal judge issued a preliminary injunction blocking their attempted takeover because he said that they had improperly used information obtained from a former executive VP of the company. The use of this information "created a compelling appearance of impropriety," said the judge. *The New York Times* quoted what it described as a source "close to Edelman" as saying, "This guy left the company two years ago. There's nothing he could have that's material anymore, and if he has it, and it's material, certainly the company has it and they should have disclosed it to shareholders."

Whether or not it is true of the Burlington matter, this quote suggests a couple of significant points. First, at least some takeover artists believe these people do have valuable information. Second, even if they've been away from the company for a while, they may still be in touch with key people who are there. By connecting with the outcasts, you may be plugging into their intelligence network. Furthermore, many fired or early-retired executives have one significant trait—time on their hands. They may suddenly be approachable, as they never were when they were in the company. So grapevining finds us jobs and tells us when we're about to lose them. How can official information compete with that kind of track record?

The Official Story

Of course, grapevines also transmit information that lacks a basis in fact. But so can official channels such as memos, corporate press releases, even private conversations with top executives. An interesting case study of this appeared in *The Corporate Communications Report*, a newsletter for corporate PR officers specializing in institutional relations. Ernest Sando, formerly director of corporate communications for the New-York-based Flexi-Van Corporation, was kept on after David Murdoch took control of the company in 1983. "He did a real bill of goods," Sando reports, "He was very nice, very chatty and very warm and he assured us that he needed us to run the company." But Sando didn't feel things worked out that way. "What they did was just make your existence untenable. . . . They made you feel worthless to the extent that you finally couldn't take it any longer and decided you had to get out for your own well-being."

Sando illustrated this complaint with several examples. He was prohibited to talk with people in the investment community, which had previously been one of his regular activities. Advertising was cut way back. "Advertising is not something you go out and do today and don't do tomorrow. . . . You develop a plan . . . you set your strategies and goals. You have to stay with it; you can't turn it on and off." He didn't even write his own press releases anymore. "The executive vice president would come to me with the press release he had written and tell me to put it out," reported Sando. He was particularly "mortified" when the company sold a major division and didn't even bother telling him about it. Analysts phoned him and he hadn't heard about it. This was embarrassing. Often when PR people claim they haven't heard of something, they're lying. But this was the truth!

Sando wasn't the only one snookered by official information. Apparently quite a few newspeople at CBS News were as well. And if these people, who are among the best and most talented news sleuths in the world, can be doubletalked, anybody can. The story begins with Ivan Boesky, the man at the center of the illegal grapevine, who in March 1985 increased his piece of CBS to 8.7 percent. Ted Turner, the CEO of Turner Broadcasting System (TBS), which owns Cable News Network, then offered to buy all of CBS's 29.7 million outstanding shares of common stock. Turner planned to pay for them with $5.4 million in junk bonds. CBS turned Turner down and then sued, asserting that TBS materially misstated the facts of its earnings in SEC filings. After months of legal maneuvers, CBS produced its own recapitalization plan, which involved buying back 21 percent of its outstanding stock for $150 per share. The cost to CBS would be nearly $1 billion. After some more legal dancing, Ted Turner tendered the CBS stock he had bought, getting paid off under the recapitalization plan. He then withdrew his own offer to buy CBS.

Next came the "restructuring." CBS sold off assets to get $300 million, after taxes, and announced that annual expenses would be cut by $20 million. Then 2,000 employees were given early retirement. The first layoff at CBS news occurred—74 employees got pushed out. Then another 51 news jobs were scrapped through more early retirements and vacancies left unfilled.

Following this, a shake-up at the top of CBS brought Laurence Tisch in as CEO. This move was endorsed by the people at CBS

News. This is when the snookering apparently began. According to an article in *The New York Times* by Peter J. Boyer, the president of CBS News, Howard Stringer, "repeatedly assured his staff that he had been promised that CBS News, which had already been through two rounds of layoffs in a year, would be spared the drastic measures applied to other parts of CBS." These assurances apparently were coming right from the top. According to the Boyer article, "At a meeting with his Washington bureau last fall, Mr. Stringer told staff members that Mr. Tisch expected economies at the news division, and that some positions would be lost through attrition. But he said he had been promised by Mr. Tisch that there would be no new layoffs at CBS News through 1987." This, of course, would have the effect of not scaring top people into fleeing to other, maybe even better, jobs.

The best news people in the business, with years of honing their suspicions and cynicism, may have fallen for it. On March 4, 1987, Stringer announced he had given Tisch a plan to scrap over 200 news jobs. The exact number of those given the boot turned out to be 215, including 14 on-air reporters. Some famous names turned up on the shaft list. Ike Pappas, on the air for 22 years, was now off. For him, the firing was an especially hard blow. Although his job had been in Washington, he was in New York because the Greek Orthodox Church was throwing a big do in his honor. Jimmy Carter would be there to honor Pappas as a Greek-American who had done well for the country and himself. Twenty members of Pappas' family were in town for the festivities.

Obviously, these news people, whose job is to ferret out the truth, knew that something was up. They knew that Stringer had been meeting for the previous few weeks with top staff people from CBS News and with consultants on efficiency from Coopers and Lybrand. The idea was to set up a cheaper operation.

This is what the "restructuring" came down to: CBS News had been divided into specific groups according to which show people worked on. The "Evening News" had the biggest staff. But the other shows also had their staffs. The restructuring would pull all of these separate groups together under a single "news czar." Dan Rather, the anchor for the "Evening News," wasn't happy about this change:

> I have worked as hard as I know how to express my deep concerns to the leadership of the news division and to the leadership of the corporation. I am deeply concerned about a number of things that are happening here. There is a restructuring of CBS News under way. The restruc-

turing is not in the direction of increasing resources to "CBS Evening News," it's decreasing. I'm concerned about that.

Tisch's comment on Rather's remarks? "I don't know anything about any reservations," Tisch said.

Andy Rooney, of "60 Minutes," said, "This guy Tisch put his money in this company; but I put my life into the company, and so did Ike Pappas and so did a lot of other people.... I own that company. Tisch does not own that company. That's the way I feel. It's Ike's company more than it is Tisch's company."

Of course, that's not the way the ownership laws read, and Tisch obliquely pointed this out. He said, "A lot of these people are lucky to be laid off right now because there are other jobs available in broadcasting."

Mike Wallace, one of the best investigative reporters there is, seemed somewhat surprised by events. Tisch's first social action as head of the network was to go to Wallace's wedding reception. Wallace said, after the cuts, "I believed then, and I believe now that Larry cares very much about the news division. Having said that, I'd like to better understand from him what he has in mind. The cuts have gone somewhat deeper than I had expected. And I think that a few of us would like to better understand where he's heading."

The events at CBS are anything but an isolated occurrence. Something strikingly analogous, although without layoffs, happened at no less a corporation than IBM. This has been rated as an "excellent" company in Peters's and Waterman's *In Search of Excellence* and has been highly touted elsewhere as well, for example, in *The 100 Best Companies to Work for in America*. According to this book, one of IBM's "cornerstones" is "*Respect for the Individual.* Caring about the dignity and rights of each person in the corporation, and not just when it is convenient or expedient to do so."

Virtually all commentators assert that IBM really is a fine place to work and that one can count on what top management says. Their official story isn't alleged to be merely a story, but the truth. So the events at the Rolm Corporation in Santa Clara, California, must have come as quite a surprise to the managers. When IBM took over their company in 1984, they had every reason to believe the promises of IBM's vice chairman, Paul J. Rizzo. He said, "Your company will be managed as a separate organization with its own character and its own culture." This remark wasn't made casually. He didn't say it after accidentally bumping into a Rolm executive in the parking lot. He made the remark at a huge outdoor meeting at Rolm for its employees. The CEO of IBM, John Akers, was sitting right there and he didn't wince, look away in embarrassment, or smile slyly. Rizzo even elaborated, asserting that Rolm's managers would continue "as a separate team."

Why were these public pronouncements made? Rumors. The grapevine at Rolm said that executives there would be forced to accept the IBM ways—including the dark blue suit, starched white shirt look.

With an official story like this from a source like this, how could you go wrong? But in March 1987, IBM announced it was integrating Rolm's marketing set-up into IBM's. This accounted for 60 percent of Rolm's 10,000 employees. One consultant, Howard Anderson, president of a Boston telecommunications consulting company, the Yankee Group, forecast that there would be a lot of Rolm employees looking for work elsewhere. The founder of Rolm, Ken Oshman, had left the year before. Anderson said the IBM action amounted to "complete integration." How could IBM have gone back on its official story? A spokesman, Adrianne C. Singer, explained, "A lot changes quickly in high-technology industries."

Price Pritchett has an interesting comment on the sort of thing that happened at CBS and IBM:

> It is ironic that top management probably never does try harder to be so truthful than it does in the merger/acquisition arena, and yet still fails. There should be little doubt that top management genuinely wants to tell the truth. But frequently executives may not know what the truth is and, as a result, catch themselves (or get caught) in duplicity. It is important to remember the employees commonly are not feeling very congenial toward the owners and top executives after the announcement that an acquisition is forthcoming. Employees are expecting more trouble. And they are expecting more surprises from the people in charge. Furthermore, when the top executives talk, everyone else in the organization hangs on their every word. It is easy for the boss to make communications mistakes.

So much for the reliability of information that comes through the official channels, which brings us back to the grapevine. How reliable is it? Studies routinely cited in management textbooks claim to show that as much as 95 percent of what travels over the grapevine is accurate. If this number is true, and we want to believe the raiders who are setting the whole nightmare in motion to begin with, the grapevine may be conveying more truthful information than the data in many corporate annual reports.

The grapevine also brings information directly into the awareness of those who need it or can use it the most, which makes it much more efficient than official announcements that go out to wide audiences, most of whom pay no attention to them.

So if anyone poo-poos the grapevine to you, check to make sure you still have your wallet.

However, when a takeover gets rolling, pieces of the grapevine get rotten. As Phillips CEO Pete Silas put it, "Don't believe everything you hear, listen to all advice you get—there's good advice and bad advice—you still have to have your own business instincts to separate the good advice from the bad."

The usual way to do this, in the absence of confirming data, is to consider the source. But according to Silas, this is precisely what you can't do once the merger scare sets in. "You can't bet on people; they may have bad information as the basis for their advice," he warns.

The Rumors After the Deal, and How to Assess Them

One type of rumor has already been discussed in the context of CBS after Tisch and the IBM takeover of Rolm—what will things be like? As we've seen in the Rolm story, the rumors of dark blue suits turned out to be right and the official story of independence wrong. And at CBS Tisch did not turn out to be viewed by the newspeople as a friend of the News division despite the fact that many of them had initially held the opposite belief.

One former CBS News producer found himself thrown onto a suddenly flooded market when he was laid off with the rest. He described in an interview the initial euphoria when Tisch took over: "There was such incredible turmoil, after Boesky and Turner, for two years. You wanted a happy ending, but I see now that in your own personal life, if it seems too good to be true, it probably is."

He reported that there had been no significant rumors at the time that Tisch would mean bad news. But there was one story based on Tisch's treatment of Loew's Hotels, one of his earlier acquisitions:

> A friend, a PR woman not at CBS, who knows Tisch from Loew's Hotels, said going to Loew's corporate headquar-

ters here in New York was like going to a Holiday Inn in Des Moines—crummy, tacky, a skeleton staff—the exact opposite of Mr. Paley with his elegant and stylish high standards. Mr. Paley was concerned up and down with a sense of style. He even had the memo pads designed with an elegant logo.

So, although the rumors were by and large positive about Tisch, they didn't square with his own manner of being. This illustrates an important way to assess rumors: *Don't go by their content, make an assessment of the nature of who has taken over, and go by that.*

The main rumors at CBS correctly said that Tisch was a firm believer in the "lean and mean" school of post-takeover behavior, which inevitably indicates that people will get canned. However, there was a contradictory rumor that CBS News would be the exception. The major rumors of "lean and mean" could easily be confirmed. One only had to walk over to Loew's corporate headquarters and look around. But there was nothing to confirm the contrary rumor about CBS News except a lot of wishful thinking.

If he really is a "lean and mean" type, the way to make a good impression is to show him that one is also "lean and mean." Interestingly, the newspeople did exactly the opposite just after Tisch took over. He and Howard Stringer went on a world tour of CBS news facilities. At each location, producers and others are reported to have come up to him and said, "I have all these stories, but I can't get them on the air." These producers thought they were lobbying on their own behalf, showing that they had been frustrated by cheap budgets. But the man with the lean and mean view simply got a cumulative effect that he had too many news people. He is reputed to have looked at CNN, noted that they got by on less, and wondered why he couldn't too.

"The information we got was a smokescreen," said the laid-off producer, adding, "He said he wanted to protect the news and cut back the fat." This producer added, from hard-won hindsight, another key point in assessing rumors: "The mistake we made was thinking he understood the news business. CBS was famous for 'the deep bench,' a term from football—the first string is good, and so is the second string. In a crisis, everyone can get out there to put the news on. I've been proud to work at CBS, working with quality people."

So a second important way to assess rumors, either favorable or unfavorable ones, is to ask, "What does the new person at the top *know about the business you're in?*" If the answer is "Not much," you shouldn't put a lot of trust in assurances that things won't change for the worse. "I guess I've learned that when the new guy comes in and says I'm not going to change anything, don't believe him," said the news producer, who added, "My show, 'Sunday Morning,' was a classy show that made money, $5 million per year for the last couple of years, and was profitable before that too. But Tisch wanted it to make more money."

One place to look for an assessment of what the new masters know about your business is Wall Street analysts. But even here, the reports will inevitably be mixed. Tisch's cuts, for example, were slammed by a First Boston Corporation media analyst, Richard J. MacDonald, who said that CBS News "defines what CBS stands for.... The ultimate Wall Street logic is you fire everyone at the network and take your programming off the air." After the cuts, MacDonald lowered his rating of CBS's stock. "They're not going to invest enough money in programming to sustain their audience," he said, adding, "They're going to let Ted Turner and the others take over." MacDonald had listed it as "buy," but changed this to "hold."

On the other hand, Bill Miller, a manager of Legg Mason Wood Walker Inc., which has a $6 million position in CBS, agreed with the cuts, although not how they were done. Miller was quoted as saying, "He would have been better off and more effective if he had said, 'We're going to look at CBS News with an eye to being efficient.'"

So the thing to do, from the standpoint of analyzing rumors and official stories, is to get the assessments of a number of Wall Street analysts, and unless they are overwhelmingly favorable to you, assume the worst about the new masters. This was the conclusion of the laid-off producer: "Assume a takeover is not going to be good for a little fish that is swallowed up. Should I have gone out and found a job a year ago? I loved what I was doing and kept doing it, but I'm not a political shark."

Shark Patrol

One thing you can do, assuming you aren't a shark yourself, is to keep your eyes glued on top managers who are. If you see their dorsal fins suddenly disappear into the distance, you might go for a long swim yourself. This is precisely what happened to the 37-year-old director of financial controls and operations at a fragrance company with $20 million in sales. He knew his company had not taken strides to increase its market share, so he was afraid it was perfect for a takeover.

After he noticed that several top honchos had quietly left, two out of choice and a third under circumstances that were never clear, he thought things might start to get tight for him too. This fear was reinforced when his secretary, a woman in her fifties who had worked for the company far longer than he had, told him, "You're next." At this point he started looking around for another job.

Shortly afterwards, his job title was changed. He was given a title he used to have, but at the same time he got a promised bonus and salary increase. This mixed signal—demotion in title but promotion in money—should, according to job counselors, be taken as a reverse of the usual belief that "money talks, bullshit walks." In this case, the words were telling the truth, the money was lying.

Why would money lie? It only has to do so for a short time. The person who has been effectively demoted has some critical information the company needs, so they don't want him to leave yet, but they do want to put him in a position in which he can't defend himself when the top managers find it convenient to ax him. After they've got whatever information they need from him, they can easily justify getting rid of him by simply getting rid of his job in their restructuring.

Often the downsizing is done before the new owners move in, so the old owners absorb the severance expense. The old top managers, with their golden parachutes, direct the executions.

A reversal of this theme happened with a 47-year-old assistant VP, the director of information systems/operations for a major bank. His area had been South America, but because of huge losses from bad loans there, his bank was scaling back its operations. However, some parts of the South American operations were to remain, and our man had critical information the bank needed.

He didn't know it, but his job at the bank had been marked for death. The trick for the bank was to make him believe that he would be kept. Demoting him in title but promoting him with money wouldn't work; he'd see through it. So the bank gave him an all-around promotion—title and money, but in the area of Latin America. This made him suspicious, since he knew what the bank's long-range plans were for that part of the world. So the bank came up with yet another ploy.

Without promising him anything additional, they sent him to their in-house language school, teaching him German and French. This allowed his ego to inflate, letting him assume that his area of operation would be expanded to include Europe as well as what was left of the South American business. Top executives encouraged this ego swelling by telling him how great he was. He began to think he was indispensable.

However, after six weeks in the language school, during which time he also helped to consolidate the South American operations, he was fired, his job eliminated altogether. The bank needed him to wrap things up in South America, and it dumped him when that was completed. Had he jumped ship earlier, he would have taken valuable information with him. These two stories contain some key lessons. First, in the turmoil of the merger, never believe what you're told unless it is completely consistent—job titles should jibe with salary, bonuses, and so forth. Second, watch out even for consistent promotions if they are in an area that you know is shaky. Third, never believe that you are indispensable, especially when the bosses hint that you are.

How Companies Fight the Main Rumors

Here are the main rumors after a takeover, according to outplacement consultants, headhunters, and managers who have had the bad luck to hear them all: who's going to get the ax; the date on which the ax will fall; and what the severance will be, if any.

A case study of how companies fight these rumors was described by Horace Scharges, now an outplacement counselor at the Manhattan firm of Bushell Cruise but formerly a VP of human resources at Management Assistance Inc., a minicomputer manufacturing company. The company was raided in a bust-up takeover by Asher Edelman, a 43-year-old who had himself transported around Manhattan in a chauffeured white jeep. Scharges and the other nine or ten top managers made out okay, getting, in some cases, two or three years' salary, benefits, plus whatever stock they had. But the other 149 staff managers started to panic, especially after Edelman announced he planned to sell off the company's two divisions, which put fear in the hearts of divisional managers too.

Scharges and 20 others were made part of the liquidation team who stayed until the end. But this left 129 other corporate staff managers who had no idea how long they'd have a job, and all the divisional people who didn't know what to expect. "We knew we'd have problems with rumors," says Scharges.

Scharges reports that he and others discussed with the corporate communications people at Gulf Oil in Pittsburgh on how they had handled rumor problems and also got advice from Towers

The Niagara of Rumors

Perrin Foster and Crosby, the largest human resource consultants in the United States.

Based on his experiences, here's what Scharges says a company should do to control rumors: tell the truth; try to anticipate rumors as much as possible within the company; play the grapevine inside and outside the company; have as many regular communications with the employees as are needed; realize that belief on the part of the employees in what the company is saying comes from constant communications from the company.

However, even applying these principles didn't quell the three main rumors. Except for rumor number one, all the staff people knew they were finished. The questions were when they'd go and how much they'd get. Since the new owners needed the staff people to close down the operation, Scharges and his colleagues had some leverage to force the owners to accept a plan giving each person a specific date when he'd be leaving and specific details of his severance. The plan was released six months before the papers on the sale of the two divisions were signed—even before Edelman and the others knew who the buyers would be for their busted-up divisions.

There was one catch: People might flee. So the plan stipulated that anyone who left before his date didn't get his severance.

Incidentally, according to Scharges, this takeover was yet another example of a healthy company being ripped apart as a result of a raid. The company's service division had been doing very well and was highly regarded in the industry. The other division, minicomputer manufacturing, did have problems, but these were being corrected with new, state-of-the-art products. These would be sold through an outstanding distribution system. The stock price simply hadn't caught up with the improvements.

Some consultants specialize in activities that inevitably lead to rumors. Office relocations are an example, and one authority on that subject is Brian A. Moran, chairman of Moran, Stahl & Boyer, Inc., an international management consulting firm headquartered in New York City that specializes in business mobility. "Decisions that affect one's personal life as well as business life are particularly stressful for managers," says Moran, adding that this is especially true of "company group moves generated by mergers or acquisitions because they are nonrecurring events, outside of normal activity."

He advises his clients to "gain credibility with affected employees through consistently timely and complete communication." According to Moran, "This is a cumulative thing, not a single stroke, that includes a variety of vehicles such as internal memos and newsletters, information centers and press releases."

Moran points out that in many of the operations on which he's consulted there has been a tendency to keep things quiet as long as possible because the deal or the move might fall through and premature disclosure could simply stir up complications unnecessarily. It could create dissidence among management and alert the competition that something is up. However, countering the need for secrecy is the need to get a wide range of views on new plans. "The idea is not to let the cat out of the bag, but to include more people in the bag," says Moran.

The way companies accomplish this is to keep working papers away from the office. "We hand-deliver quite a few feasibility studies to the homes of the CEOs, using code names such as 'Homestead,' 'Project Blue Sky,' and 'XYZ,'" says Moran. So if you happen to get a glimpse of an envelope that looks like it was addressed by G. Gordon Liddy or Colonel Oliver North, it may not mean that the Democratic national headquarters is being bugged or hostages are being swapped for arms—events presumably remote from your life. It's more likely an office relocation or takeover feasibility study—something that may *not* be remote from your life.

Naturally, this sort of cloak-and-dagger activity can backfire. "Sometimes you attract attention by diversionary tactics," says Moran, adding, "there usually are leaks." Then what? "We advise management to have 'hip-pocket memos,'" says Moran. This is a memo prepared in anticipation of a leak and usually developed primarily for the employees. "You are trying to avoid a situation where there's a story in the press, before your employees hear it from you, and you are on the defensive," says Moran.

What's in one of these "hip-pocket memos"? Here's what Moran says:

> They are designed to acknowledge and legitimize the study under way, to develop an assurance in the employees that, in a time frame that will not disbenefit them, they will be informed and their interests will be addressed. We try not to be overly specific on dates because the company may not be able to meet those dates. But whenever it's possible to be specific, there's great value in it because it enhances your credibility.

If this sounds like the hip-pocket memo is no more than a cover story, Moran says, "There's no way to answer this." These hip-pocket memos can be triggered by more likely events than someone spotting "Project Blue Sky" on the cover of an otherwise plain brown wrapper. "Requests for data that are outside the norm of the business operation always stir speculative questions and conjecture," says Moran. For example, if top management suddenly requests a complete printout of all employees, including residence and salary, tongues in data processing or human resources may start wagging. But the kind of data requested is only one tip-off. Another giveaway is who's asking. "If the requester is going outside the usual business loop, this is another signal that something is up," says Moran.

"Hopefully," says Moran, "these cover stories don't get triggered," and when they don't Moran advises a "shift to a better prepared memo. A good tactic is to use communications at regular and short intervals instead of blockbusters, in order to develop a willingness on the part of the employees to wait for the next installment as well as a confidence in and dependence on management as *the* source of information."

One device Moran has recommended in the past, but no longer does, is setting up information hotlines:

> They don't work very well because the majority of the questions asked are very specific. However, early on when hotlines make sense, these answers aren't available. People can feel frustrated because they're getting a lot of generalities. This makes them more critical of management. It would have been better for management to say "We'll tell you as much as we can as early as we can."

Based on this analysis, we have an answer to the question "How do companies fight rumors?" Self-servingly. So, for the manager caught up in these ordeals, the answer might also be to act self-servingly. One way to do that is to set up your own grapevine.

How to Network

How do you network outside of the organization? Horace Scharges, the outplacement consultant with Bushell Cruise in New York City, has counseled hundreds of laid-off managers in this art. "Don't think about people, break your life into categories," he advises. By this he means making separate lists of those you know from different activities. One list will obviously be from your business and professional life; another will be from your university; and still another may be from your church or synagogue. Some will be from fraternal organizations such as the Masons and public service organizations, such as the United Way. Political clubs can also be handy for these lists.

Once you've listed the names of people you know you can call, start with the list with the largest number of names—the more people, the more additional names they can give you.

When you call, don't even hint that you expect them to give you a job or have one for you. Here's the pitch Scharges recommends: "I'd like to come in to explain my situation, leave a copy of my resumé, and see if you might give me a few names of people who might help me with my search."

What if they won't see you? "Deal over the phone," advises Scharges, adding, "Ask if they know of anyone." This requires nerve, of course, but hard times are not the times to be shy.

KEY POINTS

- Don't trust anyone or anything at face value.
- Listen to the existing grapevine and cultivate contacts from cleaning people to former executives from your company.
- Always ask people on the outside of your company whether they've heard anything contrary to what you've been told inside the company.
- Be very suspicious of official pronouncements, no matter how reliable they've been in the past.
- Always look for another position. Rather than spending too much time "rumoring," use the time to get your resumé together and build up contacts on the outside.

2
THE SECOND ORDEAL
Who Are These Guys?

With the rumors roaring in your ear, you may now be desperate to know one thing—just who are these people who are taking over? Of course, you'll find out—eventually. You'll meet them at orientation sessions, see first hand how they operate on the job, read and reply to their memos, and find out whether they are the kind of people you can trust, the honest kind.

They may well be. But what if they're not? What if they're hatchet men, draining you of whatever useful information you have before they dump you? What if, in the worst case, they're literally crooks? By contrast, these people could be the best thing that ever happened to you, so you wouldn't want to louse up the relationship by approaching them with a suspicious attitude. Worrying about these possibilities can be very stressful, and it becomes the second ordeal of the takeover.

If you were starting a new job, you'd want to find out what you could about the people there before putting yourself at risk. Getting new bosses after a takeover is essentially the same situation, except with greater exposure because you're already a potential sitting duck. The trick is to get some useful information about your bosses before you run away from a good job or hang onto a disastrous one.

Sometimes the information problem is easy to solve.

If the new top man is a noted hatchet man, your questions are essentially answered. He's someone who is very likely to fire you.

You Can Conduct Your Own Research

But what if the new owner is not as well known? How do you find out about him? You could do a computer search of the new parent company, or of the new CEO, or both; a number of managers interviewed for this book have done just that. Where do you do this? Many local library systems offer this service at their main branches. In New York City, for example, the Queensborough Public Library very generously offers the service free to anyone with a New York City mailing address. What you get is a list of abstracts of articles, some of them in magazines geared to specific occupations. An example is *Communication World*, which runs articles about people in public relations. Then you have to track down the specific article in the library stacks or on microfilm. Another source is trade magazines.

After learning about other specific takeovers this company or CEO have accomplished, you could even do your own research into the matter. You could phone the local newspaper and ask to speak to the business editor. He might have covered the takeover and might be willing to send you some clippings or simply tell you over the phone what he knows about what happened. He might even steer you to former managers from the company who are now in other firms or in other lines of work altogether, and who could relay to you their firsthand experiences of the takeover. The danger in phoning people you don't know is that it could get back to the boss, so you might be wise to couch it in terms of the now respectable institution of networking.

The assumption here is that the boss, far from learning from his previous mistakes, will attempt to justify them in his own mind by repeating them over and over. As we'll see in the next chapter, there is a great deal of evidence that this is usually the story. Of course, newspaper clippings will probably only tell you about the top man; they won't even mention the person who may become your immediate boss or one boss above your boss. But assuming that the top man will put in place people who will give him what he wants, you can get a pretty good idea of what to expect.

Not everyone agrees that you should even try to get outside assessments of what to expect from your new bosses. San Francisco-based executive search consultant Leon A. Farley, who has consulted on a number of mergers, some of them quite large, advises strongly against it. "It is counterproductive to use research techniques to find out who your new boss is," says Farley, whose company has offices in Dallas and Washington. Then how do you find out about the new boss? "Just ask him directly," advises Farley. The assumption here is that the question is legitimate, it is likely to be recognized as such, and the person who asks it will be recognized as straightforward, but will not then be sent straight to the door. Farley advises that you put your effort into the opposite side of the issue, presenting yourself to the new boss in as honest and clear a way as possible. "The fundamental job of a good manager is to run as tight an operation as he can and to pursue a critical function," says Farley. So he suggests two key questions to ask about yourself: First, do I form an economically significant (as viewed by the new owner) function in the new business? Second, what are the intentions of the new owner?

The problem with these two questions is that they both require some understanding of what's on the new owner's mind, and that is precisely what he often does not reveal immediately, either because he doesn't really know himself or because he doesn't want you to know, as we have seen in the chapter on rumors. So this brings us back to the question, "Who are these guys?"

How do you find out about your boss once he or she has turned up to oversee you? You could do your own private investigation. Printed information might be helpful. The phone book would tell you the neighborhood your boss lives in, which could give you a lead on someone you know in the area. And this person, or someone to whom he or she refers you, could give you an idea of the sort of person your new boss is. Nice? Hard to deal with? Honest? Of course, this might only tell you what he's like outside of work—revealing, but not necessarily to the immediate point.

To find out what he's been like on the job, start with the local Chamber of Commerce. They might list his previous job titles and service organizations to which he belongs. *Who's Who* in the region might give a little on his background, including which school he went to. With this information, you could check out alumni organizations. You could contact the professional organizations to which he might belong. None of these people is likely to give negative information, but you might get leads for further inquiries.

Should You Make Use of Third Parties?

But what do you say when you speak to these people? According to John Artise, a freelance outplacement counselor who has advised people at TWA, Chase Manhattan Bank, American Airlines, and other big companies, you might do what the executive search consultants often do. "Identify yourself as writing a bio for a professional organization, and never give your real name or phone number. If you can, ask a friend to do it—a salesperson who does cold calling might work fine," says Artise.

If the third party you line up calls your own company, he must *not* identify himself as being from a prospective employer. This could get the new boss fired, which could be self-defeating since he may well plan to keep you on the payroll.

Paul W. Barada, of Barada Associates, Inc., Rushville, Indiana, runs a business doing reference checking for companies and doesn't think this sort of investigation is a hot idea. "It's a very unethical thing to do and certainly not a way to begin a relationship with a new boss.... We certainly would never do that in our reference checking," says Barada, adding, "I think the risks are far greater than any benefits you could receive from peeking in the back door. I wouldn't encourage a third party to do this since it starts off the relationship in an underhanded way, and this will probably show."

Maybe so, but Artise recommends it to bumped managers when they go through his outplacement counseling, just to make sure they don't end up in the clutches of a vulture on their next job. "I urge people to do this, absolutely," says Artise, adding, "what you're doing is the opposite of what they do to you. Otherwise you wouldn't learn the bad stuff until it's too late."

The investigation may well put you at ease so that you can be more trusting of your new boss. "I did this sort of search on my new boss," says Artise, "and I found out he was a nice guy." The assumption here is that hatchetmen build on their previous credits, as do most of us.

Artise also advises contacting headhunters, since many of them may have known about the search for your new boss, if there was one, or about past searches. He might well be in their files. Why should they tell you anything? Offer a trade. You could offer to tip them to other executives who might be looking to move. According to Artise, the search consultants have to do exactly what you would be doing just to make sure they don't place a turkey. If they don't find out in time, they jeopardize their own credibility.

But do headhunters really do this sort of sneaking-around investigation, finding out about a job candidate without his knowledge? Robert Montgomery, president, in 1987, of the Association of Executive Search Consultants, and managing partner of his own firm, Christenson and Montgomery, says he doesn't. "We have high levels of respect for the candidate's privacy and usually get written permission to conduct all references," Montgomery wrote in his association's newsletter. In an interview, he added, "During the *sourcing aspect* of the search, if someone provides a name to me, I may ask two or three easy questions—to make sure the proposed candidate is truly someone I should be pursuing. You find that a lot of referrals are out-of-work, or even in-work, golfing buddies."

Montgomery argues that a good reference checker doesn't need to sneak around. "The phone call made without the candidate's knowledge isn't going to yield more information than the call made with the candidate's knowledge—if the interviewer has the important . . . ability to conduct a reference investigation," argues Montgomery. He typically interviews 11 or 12 references, so he can get an idea of consistency.

Do candidates he lines up for jobs investigate their prospective bosses? "I have a feeling that candidates are referencing their future employers more than we know of," says Montgomery, adding, "I don't know that there's anything wrong with a person making a call to a friend in another company—it can't affect the career of the person he's looking into."

This would apply equally well to a middle manager in a taken-over company who phones a friend at the company from which his new boss has just emerged. But what about lining up a third party to make the call so you are protected from possible discovery? "I think that's deceptive and unethical," says Montgomery. "If one retains (pays) a third party, it now becomes a formal investigation and the rules of referencing should apply. That is very different from casual hearsay in the marketplace."

What about the ultimate example of this, hiring a private detective to check out the new boss? Farfetched? Maybe, but it has crossed the minds of a number of people interviewed for this book, although none has reported doing it. "I've thought time and again it would be a good idea," says Robert Half, executive recruiter and author of several books on getting a job. Half, however, discourages doing anything underhanded. "I'd tell them I was investigating," he adds. "I'd say something like, 'My references are impeccable. I hope you don't mind if I check out your company as well, because I hope we will be together for many years.'"

Does this sort of investigation violate restrictions imposed by federal law, or does it open you to the tort of invasion of privacy? It depends on how you do it. The legislation covering this issue is the Federal Fair Credit Reporting Act, which is very broadly drawn and, despite its name, not restricted to questions of paying off debt. According to Wanda L. Ellert, a labor lawyer formerly with Proskauer

Rose Goetz and Mendelsohn, a firm in New York that normally represents corporations, there is a four-part test to decide whether or not you are covered under this law. Ms. Ellert spelled it out in the newsletter of the Association of Executive Search Consultants, because, she said in an interview, many headhunters may have been unaware of this law:

> Such an agency is one that (a) acts for monetary fees, dues, or on a cooperative nonprofit basis; (b) regularly engages, in whole or in part, in gathering or evaluating any of the specified types of information on individuals; (c) distributes the information to third parties engaged in commerce; and (d) the agency must use a facility of interstate commerce to prepare or distribute the reports.

If you conduct an investigation for your own private information, you aren't doing it for a fee, as do headhunters, aren't doing it regularly, as they do, and aren't passing on the information to anyone else, as they must do as part of their work. So you should be okay under the federal law, even if some of *them* may not be. But the state laws vary and may be more restrictive, so you should check.

What if you use a phony name or cover story during your checking? "I think it would be somewhat unethical," said Ms. Ellert. But she added that it may well be legal providing you aren't passing yourself off as a cop. However, she cautioned against repeating stories that might injure someone's reputation. In this case you could be slammed with a lawsuit for invasion of privacy or intentional infliction of harm. What about using a third party to do your checking for you? "That's okay unless the friend comes under the Fair Credit Reporting Act," said Ms. Ellert.

Pay Attention at Meetings

One potential source of information on new bosses is the meetings they arrange. One middle manager, Joyce, 41, worked at a large company in the food industry when it was taken over by a competitor. She described the first of these meetings:

> Everyone was invited to the marriage ceremony—this was the metaphor top management used—a meeting of on-site employees from blue collar to executive VPs. It was elaborately done; the corporate headquarters had a lovely courtyard where this was held. The new CEO flew

out with his advisors. The whole thing was festively maudlin, since everyone sat down expecting the worst, since at our company the grapevine was more efficient than any memos.

People were there using their veracity barometers. The best part was after the official speeches when people got into little clumps and talked about how this guy or that tried to put it over. There were three discernible groups: (1) those who believed the speeches; (2) those who were willing to suspend their good intuitive understanding in pursuit of the rational judgment—in other words they didn't go with their gut when they could and I think should have; (3) those who were skeptics, who didn't believe any of it. I was one of them because in my position I knew that what was being said wasn't really true. But I had to play the role of keeping people calm.

The speakers never really lied. The circumstances and the context were set up to help people develop a sense of trust, to beguile them into nonanalysis, into procrastinating action, the extreme opposite of what you want to happen in business. They beguiled you into a false sense of hope, into a sense of inertness.

If the information in these marriage ceremony meetings isn't particularly useful, what about later meetings? "After the big marriage ceremony, they do regional dog-and-pony shows basically repeating the same thing as at the marriage ceremony," said Joyce. The "information" may have been useless, but the people doing the presentations weren't. "This is where you try to get one of the new people to notice you," said Joyce.

But which one do you target? Answering this question brings us back to the network. Some managers in your taken-over company will know people in the acquiring company just from doing business. They may know them as competitors, which will be quite common among those in marketing. Maybe they'll know them from professional associations, which opens up the exposure to staff people, or they'll know them from training programs. Often companies will send two or three people to a training program, and there may be two or three others in the same seminar from what may someday be the acquiring company. This avenue opens up potential contacts to virtually anyone in your organization. By asking around, you'll very likely find someone who knows some of these managers showing up at the regional meeting, and you'll hear which ones are okay and which ones should be avoided at all costs.

This is what happened to Joyce. People in her network pointed her to one fairly decent woman, a department head who had done some of the regional presentations. Joyce's boss then arranged an interview for her. "Once you've targeted the person, try to get him or her to be a messenger to the ax man, to say that you're worth interviewing instead of automatically axing," she said. This is precisely what happened, and Joyce was offered a job in the new set-up. However, she left after deciding she didn't like the way the new company did things.

Sometimes the meetings are neither marriage ceremony nor dog-and-pony show; they are more like Kiwanis Club dinners, where executives from comparable divisions in the two companies join each other at big round tables for good-natured dinners, where people are supposed to kid each other and laugh. So there you are, staring across the table at your opposite number. You know that although there may be enough chairs for both of you at this table, back at the office there will only be one chair, so one of you will be having dinner elsewhere when the next shindig is held. At least here's a chance to get the measure of your opposite number, see how much of a pal he appears to be with the top brass. One thing you may not do at these functions is trip him when he's going down the stairs. "Everybody is very friendly at these things, because at this point you need friends," reported one manager who had eaten several of these dinners.

Why Your New Bosses May Not Know What They're Doing

One thing is extremely likely about the new managers—they may not know what they're doing. This is an all too common phenomenon that is built right into the deal itself—a fact that has been shown in the research of David Jemison and Sim Sitkin, writing in the *Harvard Business Review*. They interviewed over two dozen top executives, investment bankers, and consultants involved in making takeover deals, and found three basic characteristics of the negotiations that tend to gum up the works, almost guaranteeing that things will be a mess later when people who actually do the work at the merged company try to get down to it.

Deal Makers Are Not Operating Managers

Lawyers, bankers, accountants, consultants, and various other number crunchers and loophole manufacturers dominate the negotiations. Each of them is well paid and often the best at his trade. They have one eye, and maybe both eyes, on potential lawsuits. So they do things that can be justified on paper. This means that numerical and legalistic data about products, markets, industries, technologies, patents, properties, and so forth dominate the discussion. Standard methods of financial evaluation are what they rely on. Some of these guys may not like the term "asset stripper," but they certainly keep their focus on the tangible assets. As Jemison and Sitkin wrote, "The investment bankers we interviewed told us that they rely chiefly on calculations based on purely quantitative criteria that can more easily be defended if challenged legally."

What this comes down to is that the people who make the deal often are not responsible for making its results work. So if an operating manager gets in the room, it's often by mistake. The CEO, of course, may have once been an operating manager, but now he's operating as a deal maker, and he has to put together a team of people fast. These people often have not worked together before, don't know each other, don't even know the jargon that each one spouts.

So one way to figure out in advance whether your new bosses know what they're doing is to find out the answer to one simple question: *Were the operating managers who will be responsible for actually running the operations present during most or all of the negotiations?* If not, there's a pretty good chance the deal is being put together and pushed by asset strippers, who plan ultimately to bust up the company, or by top executives showing reckless disregard for the consequences of the business as a going concern. In this case, hard-working, sincere managers are almost guaranteed trouble.

Deals Are Closed Fast

Another thing to look for, according to Jemison and Sitkin, is how fast the deal was made. If it was something like overnight, the odds increase that your new bosses don't know which end is up.

Merger deals have their own dynamic, with a lot of pressure to close fast. If top management succumbs to that pressure, you, as a hard working manager, are in for trouble. What are the pressures? One is the stock market. If the deal has leaked to the press, the top people are under tremendous pressure to do something because of stock market and other uncertainties. Since it will almost inevitably leak, they must work fast. And after news does leak, they have to work even faster.

Another pressure is psychological. Without exception, people interviewed for this book who negotiated takeover deals have described how staggeringly intense the experience was. Cathy Rein, former corporate counsel for the Continental Group, who was at the center of the negotiations that led to the absorption of her company by a White Knight, said in an interview, "It was the most fun I've ever had in my career, even though I was working myself out of a job." Jemison and Sitkin quoted Warren Buffett, chairman of Berkshire Hathaway: "Managerial intellect wilted in competition with managerial adrenalin. The thrill of the chase blinded pursuers to the consequences of the catch." But generals often find war exciting. Why shouldn't they? They get to make the big decisions and then watch while lesser mortals prove their mortality.

So one thing to look for during the negotiation is reports that the negotiators are loving every second of it. If so, remember you'll be the foot soldier they'll later look at through the periscope from the safety of their bunker.

The boss's excitement does have a price, however. How can a senior executive put all this energy into a deal and then fail to make it? He's entrapped by his own earlier decision to go after the target in the first place. So he may make the deal even when some honest person on the negotiation team tells him the deal isn't such a hot one. The pressure may well be on to ignore the bad news.

In addition to the irrational incentive to close, which at least is mildly understandable, even if disastrous to your career as a manager, there's a much more sinister incentive—careerism and appalling greed on the part of allegedly disinterested participants. So another question to research is: *Who's on the negotiation team and what's in it for them if the deal goes through?* Here's what could be in it for them: time spent with the CEO, bonuses and promotions for identifying and then closing the deal on an acquisition, or a move from staff to line authority, even to top management, in the acquisition.

One group whose incentives are easy to figure out are the investment bankers. They get paid a piece of the deal, and it's the same amount whether they make the deal in five minutes or five months. Which do you think they'd prefer?

Of course, if there's no deal at all, then the investment bankers don't get paid the same amount. Jemison and Sitkin quote Felix Rohatyn of Lazard Freres on this: "Fees are sometimes ten times as large when a deal closes as when it doesn't, so you'd about have to be a saint not to be affected by the numbers involved . . . the level of fees has reached a point that . . . invites suspicion that there's too much incentive to do a deal." Where's the worry in this of integrating the two companies after the deal is made? There isn't any. The incentive is *literally* to be irresponsible on the part of those who push the deal, because they are literally not responsible for the consequences.

These irrational reasons for making the deal help to explain why the new managers commonly fire floors full of managers; they do it as a way of covering their backsides. If they can fire a lot of people, then they can get away with saying, "Look at the mess we found, it may take us some time to set things straight around here." But if they don't start with wholesale slaughter, they may not be able to pass the blame onto others. Incidentally, the ruthless blame-passers probably don't deserve the blame themselves because they weren't in on the deal-making either.

Issues Are Left Unresolved

The third characteristic of the deal that helps to make it all too likely that your new boss won't know what he's doing is the deliberately unresolved ambiguity in the deal. This is a standard negotiation tactic, used, for example, in treaty negotiations between countries. The tough issues are put off for future negotiations, the easier ones wrapped up and put into a partial agreement. For example, the underground nuclear test ban treaty between the United States and the Soviet Union left all other issues of the arms race, which were harder to settle, out of the discussion.

But there's a catch: "One of the difficulties in settling the easier issues first is that there remain fewer opportunities for log rolling with the residue of tougher issues," according to bargaining expert Howard Raiffa of the Harvard Business School and Harvard's Kennedy School of Government.

When the United States and the Soviets put off agreement on an intractable issue, there's always—let's hope—another day to talk about it. Besides, arms negotiations are embedded in a constantly changing world of other issues that can be used for log-rolling purposes. But when a takeover or merger deal is concluded —end of story. The managers on one side have all the power, those on the other have none, except the power to walk away or to obstruct by being "passively aggressive," that is, they can use passivity as a weapon.

So whatever isn't spelled out in detail in the takeover negotiation, because it is too tough to figure out or too much of a stumbling block, is in fact implicitly resolved in favor of whatever pops into the minds of the managers who dominate the acquisition. The dominated managers, the holdovers from the old order, may not realize this implicit resolution until too late, when they suddenly feel they've been had.

What wouldn't be resolved in a takeover deal? Presumably, everything to do with money has been worked out in order to head off lawsuits. So the only matters left unresolved must have to do with people—in other words, with you. As we've seen, these are precisely the issues that could pour cold water on the whole idea of the takeover in the first place. Even if they're not really stumbling blocks, they are time consuming, and the pressure to close might prevent their resolution. So the CEOs leave them to lesser lights to work out later. Often the taken-over CEO doesn't care anyway; he bails out with his golden parachute.

Jemison and Sitkin gave an example of an unnamed consumer products company where the idea was that the acquisition would give the acquirer access to the subsidiary's markets. Sounds fine, right? Plenty of synergy there—on paper. But to get it, the marketing and sales people of the subsidiary would have to cooperate, and why should they if they figured they were just going to be pushed out the door after they'd been bled for whatever they had? Their only leverage was to hold back cooperation. Sales people might even be able to take their accounts to a new company. The acquisition flopped because the managers of the dominant company and those of the subsidiary competed with each other instead of with outside competitors.

Another version of this same sort of thing was described in an interview by a former manager in a medical equipment company that had been taken over by a huge cosmetics firm:

> We had our own leasing company—the customer could buy or lease our equipment. The rental rates hadn't gone up in a while. Once a customer rented an item, we gave him the same rate from year to year, despite an escalation clause in the contract which allowed us to raise the rates. The clause wasn't used, so the customers were happy and they stayed with us, renting other equipment from us.
>
> However, the sharpies who looked over the books during the takeover noticed these unused escalation clauses and wondered how this marvelous opportunity to squeeze the customer had been

missed. Naturally, this issue was left unresolved in the takeover negotiation. Had it been brought up, of course, the long-range business judgment of the sharpies would have been brought severely into question, and the managers of the taken-over company, who had carefully nurtured the relationship with their customers, would have screamed.

On paper these escalation clauses represented an asset. But in reality, when the clauses were exercised, large numbers of customers simply shifted to other suppliers. So the takeover company ultimately lost money.

So the third question to ask yourself, to make a reasonable assessment of whether your new bosses will know what they're doing, is: *What details about the operations were included in the merger or takeover agreement?* If the answer is "plenty," you may have reason to be optimistic. If the answer is "not enough," you can probably assume that the new bosses' ignorance of your company's operations will raise some obstacles.

KEY POINTS

- Start your research with a computerized library search on the new owners.

- Consider asking your new boss directly about himself and his background when he comes on board. Some consultants strongly advise this.

- Don't be taken in by all the backslapping and hoopla at the "marriage ceremony" meetings. You can't forget that only other people's money got married, and for now you are merely invited to the cake-cutting ceremony.

- Keep your eyes and ears open at the regional dog-and-pony shows—the dinners for specific groups of executives. You may get useful information on what you'll be facing and who might be helpful.

- Make an assessment of how the new bosses will run your company by finding out who was present when the deal was made and what was on the agenda.

3

THE THIRD ORDEAL
The Anglo Saxons versus the Normans

After two insurance companies merged, a regional manager, age 41, was fired. A lousy producer? On the contrary, he had been one of the best. Always a maverick who had previously been tolerated, he didn't fit in anymore. His problem was that he worked hard and lived modestly and did not put himself into the kind of debt that would guarantee his economic dependence. He drove a three-year-old car, instead of buying a new Porsche every year; he refused to take on a huge mortgage, unlike all the other surviving executives in the merged operation. So the insurance company fired him for having too much old fashioned virtue in his private life.

"This is the best thing for both, because of the need for matching; even though he might produce better than someone else, he'll also disrupt the system," said New York outplacement consultant James J. Gallagher, Ph.D., adding, "he wouldn't conform. The hard part was getting him to understand his own motivations and accept the fact that the new organization had the right to define its own."

For many years before the current merger epidemic, quite a few consultants have pushed the idea of "corporate culture." What's that? Here's how the *American Heritage Dictionary* defines culture: "the totality of socially transmitted behavior patterns, arts, beliefs, institutions, and all other products of human work and thought characteristic of a community or population." A former managing director of McKinsey and Company gave a quick definition of corporate culture: "the way we do things around here."

In other words, some consultants have advocated the idea of consistency and helped top management to achieve it. Then comes the takeover.

Writing in *Psychology Today*, two consultants on the post-merger situation said: "We have often seen at this time what psychologist Amy Sales of Boston University has termed a 'clash of cultures.' People start to focus upon the differences in the way the two companies operate and are managed." Often, those in the taken-over company describe themselves as a conquered people, like the Anglo Saxons after the Norman conquest. Naturally, they resent the executives sent to oversee them, often viewing them as heartless tax collectors for absentee owners.

The consultants continued: "In one case we studied, executives in one company saw themselves as being participative and people-oriented while they viewed their counterparts as autocratic numbers people."

There it is, the Anglo Saxons forced to fill in the Normans' "Doomsday Book." (This was the count William the Conqueror ordered of people and property in England after he took over the place. William was the original number cruncher.) Nearly everybody caught up in mergers reports this clash of Anglo Saxons against the Normans. The typical, but apparently not inexorable, pattern seems to be that the people taken over genuinely don't like their new bosses and the new bosses feel superiority over, and thus contempt for, those who work for the company that has been bought.

The arrogance and resulting resentment can start even before the deal is made. When a major multinational, multidivisional company acquired a food service operation, an agreement on the deal was made in principle. Then the multinational sent swarms of young, freshly scrubbed MBAs to climb around the food service organization for three or four months. When the meeting was held to consummate the deal, top management of the food service company was there. But the conglomerate sent a third-level manager. Naturally, this deeply offended the top management of the acquired company. As the third-level manager presented a summary sheet of the deal, the management of the other company suddenly realized that the conglomerate had changed the offer. "This is bullshit," said the CEO of the acquired company, as he walked out. The conglomerate replied with an unfriendly takeover.

Perhaps because of the arrogance of the acquiring company, managers rarely say, "My employer was bought." They nearly always express their situation in the language of slavery: "We were bought."

There may well be fundamental differences between the way things are done in the swallowing company and the way they are done in the swallowed company. In one, the CEO may be addressed as "Mr. Caruthers," but in the other, he may simply be "Bud." In the conquering company, memos may document every spoken word. Whole forests may have been sacrificed so executives could cover their backsides. But in the company taken over memos may have been as rare as two-dollar bills.

The differences in corporate style can be quite striking. When a New York conglomerate took over a Texas package goods company, the new VP of marketing arrived and demanded a report from one of his immediate subordinates with the words, "I want this goddamn thing by six o'clock!" The subordinate, a well-mannered Texan, replied, "You can't have it by six o'clock, and kindly don't talk to me like that." The new boss said, "You'd better get used to it because that's the way I'm going to do things." "Then I quit," said the Texan. "You can't quit," replied the new boss, "I need that report by six o'clock." "Too bad," answered the Texan as he walked out the door, never to return.

Although this gentleman walked out instantly, his voluntary departure was not unusual in this and many other takeovers. In the case of the Texas package goods company, according to one manager who stayed, "More middle managers quit than were fired. The culture changed quickly and a lot of people weren't able to adapt to it."

The well-mannered Texan wasn't the only one to depart on short notice. One manager reported, "A meeting started at 8:00 A.M. There was a coffee break at 10:00 and then the meeting started back up again 15 minutes later. But some people were missing, although no one said anything. We found out later they were fired during the coffee break."

These departures, whether confrontational or amazingly sudden, may be indicative of fundamental differences between the two groups of managers. The gut questions that reveal these differences may be: How much money do these people make? Are they Protestant? Catholic? Jewish? WASP? Italian? Irish? Are they a bunch of crooks?

Why Are Those Conquerors Swaggering?

Maybe because they're making so much money. The ones strutting around the taken-over headquarters may well be "fast trackers," those marked for rapid advancement over others hired at the same time. Fast-track managers used to be those who earned their age. In other words a 30-year-old made $30,000. Forget that. We haven't quite reached the point where a fast tracker must earn his exponential age—the 30-year-old must make 30 to the 30th power—but we're heading in that direction.

According to a study by the Association of Executive Search Consultants:

> Today the hot-shot 30-year-old should be pulling in about $62,000 or more than twice their age. In addition, the ratios speed up as the years pile on. Today, a 40-year-old fast-tracker can expect to be earning approximately $132,000 or more than 3.3 times his/her age. A 45-year-old fast-tracker, at about $179,000 is earning almost 4 times his/her age.
>
> Exceptional managers are earning higher salaries earlier, and it is becoming the norm for a top-flight executive to break "Mach I"—$100,000 and more before age 40.

If this is the kind of money these people, the ones who are now overseeing your old company, are making, no wonder they're strutting around. Most of the middle managers at the acquired company have been there a while. Many are lifers, or thought they were until the takeover. They are probably not making this kind of money. If you don't believe this, hang around an outplacement office for a while and see what kinds of salaries middle managers would be perfectly happy to settle for. So those not making the big dough may resent the new overlords who, in turn, may have contempt for them. As we see, based on money alone there may be an unbridgeable gap between the two groups.

This gap hits even accountants—if they're the ones taken over. "My five partners and I felt we just couldn't mesh with the local Peat office," said Paul Allen, in a recent article in *The Wall Street Journal* by journalist Lee Burton, who is himself an expert on accounting. The article dealt with the merger of KMG Main Hurdman with Peat Marwick to form the biggest of the Big Eight, with worldwide revenue of $2.5 billion. The gentleman quoted, Mr. Allen, was the head of the Wichita, Kansas, office of KMG, the gobbled-up firm. "All six of us are native Kansans. We all started at the bottom here. The Peat partners were mostly from out of state. They had come into town with fancy salaries and big jobs," said Mr. Allen. Robin Hood might have said the same sort of thing just before he dashed into Sherwood Forest with his Merry Men to take on Prince John, the Sheriff of Nottingham, and the rest of their Norman pals.

This analogy isn't quite as farfetched as it sounds. According to the Burton article,

> Mr. Allen and his partners chose to stay small. They started their own firm. But a trail of acrimony has been left behind. A lawsuit filed in a Kansas state court last January by Mr. Allen's firm to stop the merger is still pending. And KMG Main Hurdman says Mr. Allen's firm owes it $3 million in lost client revenue—a claim that Mr. Allen denies.

Partnership mergers work differently from ordinary corporate ones, since each partner owns a piece of the business. Each can go his own way. Quite a few did. Just before the merger, KMG had 503 U.S. partners. Only 378 stayed. Peat Marwick, by contrast, had 1,399 U.S. partners before the merger, but only 33 of them left after the merger. These kinds of partners are really like a collection of feudal noblemen. William may defeat Harold at Hastings, but noblemen like Mr. Allen may not agree to this defeat—and fight it out court. John C. Burton, Columbia's dean of the Graduate Business School, was quoted in the *Journal* article comparing the partners not to feudal lords but to another remnant from the middle ages, tenured university faculty members: "It's like putting together two huge universities and combining hundreds of tenured faculty. You can't order partners or professors around. You can cajole, wheedle, and encourage. But they're very sensitive to their rights."

The Doomsday Book Writers

Suppose you're in operations in a manufacturing company and your company has just been taken over. What do you suppose are the chances that the new overseers are going to speak your language and understand the problems of manufacturing?

Pretty lousy.

According to a survey by the executive search firm, Korn/Ferry International:

- Only about 2 percent of senior management are now in production/manufacturing, although about 8 percent started out there.
- Twenty-eight percent started out in finance or accounting, and about 23 percent are still in that area.
- By contrast, nearly 18 percent started out in marketing, but only 7 percent are still there.
- The biggest group are in "general management," about 44 percent, even though less than 4 percent started out there.
- Only a little over 6 percent of the respondents are in "professional/technical" functions—including for some reason both lawyers and scientists—although almost 23 percent started there.

Here's what the Korn/Ferry survey says all this boils down to:

Obviously, those who began in finance/accounting were more likely to remain in that discipline throughout their careers *and to secure senior executive status.* Furthermore, the retention rate for this function has gone up since 1979, indicating continued success in career advancement for a large number of finance executives.

Low and dropping retention rates for marketing/sales and professional/technical executives indicate that these are the professionals who must move to general management positions in order to continue their career advancement. In fact, current top management includes only 7% marketing/sales professionals and only 6% professional/technical or personnel. Remaining within these disciplines is clearly not the way to advance for a significant number of executives. However, 23% of current senior level executives are in the finance/accounting function, the second largest group behind general management."

What this means is that the number crunchers are likely to be the ones you'll be dealing with. William the Conqueror and his Doomsday Booksters would have felt right at home with this bunch.

This emphasis on numbers can even happen when the Doomsday Booksters are literally in the book business. An example was when a publicly traded but family-run publishing company in New York City was taken over by a high-powered conglomerate, also in New York. Each part of the taken-over publishing house was required to report on its operations to the new owners. One divisional manager, David, explains what happened when he gave his pitch:

> I presented my part of the business, sales going up 17 percent a year and profits tripled in two years. This was one of the best records in the old company and I was pretty proud. So you can imagine how I felt when the manager looked at me and said, "You realize that's not good enough." I quickly said, "Of course, there's plenty of room for more growth."

One interesting thing is that this increase in power of the finance crowd seems to be reflected in an awful lot of takeovers. Philip Mirvis, a consultant who did a lengthy study of one specific White Knight takeover, which he reported under the disguised name GrandCo, wrote, "Gaining financial control was the central objective of GrandCo in this case and its strategy for the combination closely followed it. This is a common aim in conglomerate acquisitions."

Another interesting thing about the rise of the finance gang is that it precisely correlates with the rise of corporate debt, discussed in the introduction to this book. These guys may not know much about manufacturing, but they apparently know all about piling on debt, which they do in the name of *competitiveness*. What does this mean in terms of your strategy to survive the merger? You may have genuine trouble cozying up to the new guys. These Normans may not speak Anglo Saxon.

A recent McKinsey staff paper distinguishes three types of corporate cultures, basing them on a sort of economic determinism. One tends to exist in cost-driven businesses, such as those that manufacture an established product. Another can be found in service-driven businesses, such as airlines or fast food chains. The third turns up in innovation-driven businesses, producing products that are the first on the market. Each of these types requires a different kind of emphasis. For example, successful cost-driven businesses usually require flat organization structures with few staff people. The emphasis is on controls, efficiency, and speed of decisions. Service-driven businesses, according to this study, are most concerned with customer satisfaction, and managers put in a lot of time shooting the breeze with customers to get a sense of how they feel about the service. Successful innovation-driven businesses put a great deal of focus on R&D spending and are often organized into little entrepreneurial pieces. There is often a heavy emphasis on belief in the company, on an *esprit de corps*.

The punchline is that if the new parent is from one type of industry but the subsidiary is from another, there is a real possibility that the managers of the two organizations will treat each other like hostile foreigners. As the McKinsey paper puts it, "A corporate parent attempting to manage a portfolio that contains a mixture of cost-, innovation- and service-driven businesses will thus not find it easy to create a supportive organizational environment for all three."

A conglomerate's taking over a single-product company can sometimes lead to bizarre misunderstandings. When the New York City publishing house was taken over by the conglomerate there was some initial confusion over who was the boss of one division of the company taken over. David, the man quoted earlier, tells what happened:

> At one point we were called to corporate headquarters to a lunch meeting, and we thought it was with our new boss. We spent two and a half hours with him, and on the way back to the airport we said to each other "How can this be? He doesn't know anything." He eventually came out to our office and for a short time he acted as if he were the boss, telling us to go to this meeting or go to that meeting. But pretty soon we realized that he worked for *us*! But he didn't have too much to contribute, so we called the guy I report to and we got rid of him with no problems.

The holdover managers also gave some of their former brethren the same treatment. "They weren't fired by the new managers, the 'Them,' but by the 'Us,' who got fed up with those who weren't working hard," reports David.

So the "us against them" phenomenon doesn't always end up disastrously. In fact, David gives the whole takeover very high marks: "For me, this has been great. Some people haven't adapted. I have. I love it. I like it better now than before. It's a much more exciting place. If there was no reason for mergers, they should have been invented."

However, David is quick to point out that not everyone else has been so happy with the takeover. "One manager went to dinner with her new boss and thought she was home free. But two weeks later she was called in and fired. She had been too closely linked with unsuccessful product lines. In the old company she'd have been moved somewhere else, but now, she was fired."

In other takeovers, the Anglo-Saxons-against-the-Normans

phenomenon has been minimized by thoughtful managers from the parent company. When one California bank took over another, many people on the acquisition side were fired, but some entire units were brought over and integrated into the combined operation. One manager in commercial lending who had survived the takeover reported, "I was at one particular meeting when people who had always been at the acquiring bank started to lecture us on their ways of doing things. 'We do this . . . ,' he started saying, but our boss, his and mine, stopped the conversation by saying, 'We don't do anything, we're one bank now.'"

Even if some of these Normans can be quite decent, occasionally the Anglo Saxons harbor resentment for a long time. At the publishing house, David reports, "some of the people reporting to me now two and a half years later still refer to 'them.' I ask, Who is 'them?' But you still hear remarks about the good old days."

But the success stories, even with qualifications, may well be the exception. The McKinsey paper goes on to point out that since managers familiar with one kind of business may not know what they're doing in another kind of business, takeovers in new business areas usually fail. "Most of those that attempt it fail, in the end, to do as well for their stockholders as if they had simply paid out the surplus cash flows from their existing business portfolios through some combination of high dividends and periodic stock repurchases."

Another McKinsey study was quite striking. It was of 56 Fortune 200 industrials that bought unrelated businesses after 1968. The study showed that only 23 percent, 13 in all, managed to earn at least their cost of capital on money sunk into the purchase; 70 percent failed to earn their cost of capital, and 7 percent couldn't be determined one way or the other. Part of the reason for this astonishing failure rate, according to the study, has to do with the relative size of the acquisitions. The big ones tended to bomb out, but the little ones were more successful—although they still tended to fail the cost of capital test. Forty percent of the little ones succeeded, but only 16 percent of the big ones did. What's a big acquisition? In the McKinsey study, a big acquisition is one that was more than 10 percent of the buyer's equity before the acquisition. Why did the little ones work out better than the big ones? It may have something to do with corporate culture. According to the study, "To create value in the acquisition, the acquiror must change the way the acquired company does business. Changing large companies is much harder than changing small ones, and takes disproportionately more human resources and time."

McKinsey's punchline: "Reconcile yourself to the fact that, in acquisition, small is beautiful."

Ethnic Origin, Religion, Sex

What are the new bosses' most likely ethnic backgrounds? According to the Korn/Ferry survey, "As in 1979, all non-white respondents taken together still constitute less than 1% of the total." So you probably won't notice any change here.

The percentage of women responding to the survey had gone up from .5 to 2.1. So the takeover is unlikely to bring with it a wave of new female overseers. This is not exactly good news for women in middle management in the company taken over, who must now prove themselves all over again. Furthermore, they could easily be pushed out the door along with railcarloads of male managers, and not be in a strong position to make a discrimination case. The Korn/Ferry survey compares its current results with those of 1979: "Six years later, despite industry and government efforts to promote opportunities for women and minority executives, the progress in this area is minimal."

But there has been a small shift in religion over these six years. In the current survey, 58 percent of the respondents are Protestants, compared to 68 percent six years earlier. This translates into a rise in the respondents from the other two major religions in this country. "The number of Catholics has risen from 22% to 27% and the number of Jews from 6% to 7%," says the survey. Keeping in mind that the survey is not based on a scientific sample, there may nonetheless be an increase in the chance that the new overseers will not have the same religion as did the last people running your company.

Where all of this could be significant is if your company is not one of the Fortune 1000, but is taken over by one. If the ethnic background of your managers is not WASP, the odds are that those of the new overseers will be. Does this mean that they will flaunt the ethnic distinctions? Almost certainly not. But these distinctions may well play from underneath in large numbers of takeovers. "This is the sort of thing that comes out after people have had a couple of drinks and tell you what's really on their minds," said one consultant who asked not to be identified.

The Psychology of Resentment

Resentment can show up in all sorts of peculiar ways. "Often the small things cause the biggest resentment," says Dr. Arnold J.

Frigeri, formerly the director of training for a Fortune 100 corporation but now a solo consultant. "The big problems are in the small perks," he adds. For example, an acquired company may have had a standard policy of allowing even lower ranking middle managers to fly first class. But the acquiring company may be more restrictive. Even top management may have to fly in the big cabin with the ordinary folk. In one case a lower ranking manager from the acquired company took his seat in first class. On walked a top-brass number cruncher from headquarters, who said hello to the well-seated young man as he sullenly walked back to his usual seat in steerage. As he did so, he thought long and hard that the young man and his high-riding fellows in the acquired company had not yet had all of their numbers crunched. And when he got back to headquarters, he saw to it that they did.

Sometimes, although the discrepancies cause resentment in the acquiring company, the anger is at a low enough level that top management can safely ignore it in the interests of promoting harmony. An example of this happened when an aerospace conglomerate acquired a smaller aerospace company. The smaller company had an ideal MBA tuition payment program—they shelled out the money to their employees in advance, so the employee-students were going to school for free. The acquiring company was cheaper. It reimbursed its employees if they got high enough grades in the courses. The small fry at the acquiring company resented the free ride obtained by the small fry at what should have been, in their eyes, the dominated company. But the head of the company taken over made an issue of keeping things the way they were, and the CEO of the parent didn't want to take him on over a small-change issue that didn't affect himself or his immediate cronies.

A Sense of Powerlessness

But these are topics of resentment concerning the managers with the whip hand. Far greater is the resentment on the other side, at the taken-over company. For one thing, these managers often don't even use the same word to describe the transaction that put them in the stew. Whereas managers at the buying company usually call the deal an "acquisition," those at the company that was bought quite often call it a "merger." One term, of course, implies domination, the other equality. These differing terms for the same event help the managers on the two sides to dislike each other.

This dislike can show up in bizarre ways. For example, a major consulting company bought a smaller one, which was largely in market research. The two companies were totally different in their corporate ways. The big buyer was strictly grey business suits and formal manners. But the small company was more academic—tweed jackets and scholarly manners. Most had Ph.D.s in psychology. The people there were older too, and somewhat set in their ways.

The buyer had one thing in mind—fire no one. After all, the only thing they were buying was the talent of the people working there. So they sent a very amiable guy, who himself had a Ph.D. in psychology, to be the man from corporate. He had one instruction—tread lightly. He took a small office down the hall from the much larger one of the much older CEO. The new viceroy didn't even have his own secretary, but shared one with the current CEO of the small company.

This led to the crisis. The little company had one quirk in its corporate ways—everybody ate at the same corporate commissary. Very democratic, but also, according to the new viceroy, very lousy coffee. "But if that's what they wanted, fine, I just didn't want to drink the stuff," he reported. So he had the secretary fill in a requisition for a small coffee machine for himself. The older CEO found the paper in the outbasket and transferred it to the wastebasket.

This gratuitous action began a power struggle, which ended two years later when the 62-year-old CEO was ushered out the door. What is the psychology underlying this sort of resentment? According to one psychologist, Philip Mirvis, who has studied several mergers over a period of years, managers in the taken-over company feel "powerlessness and helplessness." As we've seen in instance after instance, they should feel these emotions, since there is a great deal to feel powerless and helpless about.

When Gulf+Western took over Prentice Hall, one middle manager who had been there for nearly 25 years at the time, Mary Kennan, stuck around for another year and a half. She was quoted in *Publishers Weekly* on what the postmerger situation was like. Said Kennan: "Our perception, perhaps mistaken, was that we had no real leader during that difficult period, and we began to develop a kind of concentration camp mentality. We didn't know what would happen next and began to plan week by week rather than season by season."

An analogous experience was reported in the merger of two accounting firms (not KMG and Peat Marwick). One 39-year-old who had just been made partner in the smaller firm, and in fact *wanted* the merger to take place, also felt powerless to do anything about it:

I had no control; every other day I'd hear "the deal's off, the deal's on." Even the partners who were negotiating weren't sure where they stood. Everything susceptible to negotiation could break down the deal. This went on for three months. I was so crazy, I was out of my marriage for four months, and I felt like I was going through two divorces. If this was what was going on with the partners, you could imagine what was going on with the staff.

Keep in mind that this is the remark of someone who favored the merger. The senior partners weren't so keen. "The younger partners wanted the merger to take place, but the older partners said okay, but we'll take what's due us." Like many of the older partners in the KMG-Peat Marwick merger, many of the older partners in this other merger left. They didn't like the loss of autonomy.

Part of the sense of powerlessness is the realization that without a good job at a big corporation, one literally may be powerless. One former general manager at the Continental Group, who lost his job along with virtually everyone else on the corporate staff, described this link:

> You are who you work for, to a great degree. There's a sense of belonging to a corporate family, a pride of being part of big business. Then there was the cachet and sense of identify of the circles I traveled in—the Roundtable, access to the White House. Then there were the perks that went with the job—the Concorde to Europe, staying at the George V in Paris, the Madison in Washington. Now that I'm in business for myself, I stay at the Holiday Inn.

No wonder people feel a sense of powerlessness when they see their companies no longer existing, or themselves no longer linked to the companies; the companies had given them status in the world. The self that it gave them may have been a false one, but it sufficed. The former staff manager from the Continental Group is now well aware that his former sense of self may have been questionable:

> I feel like an outsider now, sitting like any other vendor in the waiting room of a company. The first year [of] doing this business it really bothered me. Now it doesn't. For one thing, when I see these people walking around looking very busy, 90 percent is bullshit, busywork. But what I'm now doing is important; if I make the sale it's worth a lot of money. I look at them, at their arrogance, and my

attitude now is, "I've been there before, I had a better job, made more money. But I'm better off now—I'm free."

Sounds a bit like Scrooge after he sees Marley's ghost, doesn't it?

When this manager lost his corporate job, he was almost literally treated by people still holding corporate jobs as if he were not a real human being anymore. "About one quarter of the corporate people were arrogant. Some I thought were personal friends, but when I left, an invisible shield came between me and them."

Sometimes the powerlessness comes from a feeling of frustration. As we saw in the introduction, common to many mergers is the fact that companies are often taken over when they are already improving themselves but before the stock market cottons on to that fact. This can be very frustrating to managers, who like Moses, wander for 20 years in the desert, but then for one reason or another run afoul of the powers that be just before hitting paydirt. A banker who had helped to turn his bank around and then saw it sold out from under him described his feelings: "People had worked extremely hard to turn the institution around. Then there was the frustration of not being able to see the fruits of that effort."

One big source of the sense of powerlessness is that managers in the company taken over can be easily scapegoated. Whatever goes wrong can be blamed on their bad old ways. This often begins by blaming those who weren't brought along into the combined operation or who bailed out early on. A successful banker who was hired by the new parent in a takeover, and did very well afterwards, elaborated:

> People would talk down about my old bank's way of doing things. But I never came across people who talked in a personal sense, other than about those who had not been brought on and were then talked about as incompetent. Whenever there were problems, blame could easily be laid on my old bank and its ways. For a while there was a hiatus where all problems went back to my bank. For example, if there was a bad loan, people would say it wouldn't have been made by the parent bank because the people there perceived it as having a tougher credit process.
>
> This just plain isn't true. I'm the agent for a loan made by the old bank and now I'm the agent for the same loan under the new bank. People here say that the old bank was too easy on these people; they didn't buckle down on them. One of the people in the company was on the board

of directors of the old bank. So there's the perception that the old bank went easy. But I think exactly the same loan would have been given at that time by the new bank.

Since this banker has been successful, the scapegoating apparently hasn't damaged his career. But for others, who are insecure and who see blame being thrown around unfairly, there is the opportunity for resentment. The banker added, "There are people from the old bank who were brought over but have since left the new bank. Problems were found in their loan portfolios. So they got residual damage to their careers because they didn't get a good reference."

Don't make the mistake of thinking all the managers on the taken-over side are completely powerless. As we'll see in specific examples in later chapters, this is far from the case. Your power nearly always comes from your knowledge of inside poop. For example, labor relations people know the history of specific bargaining and grievance problems. As long as they don't give this information to the new owners, they are nearly indispensable if the company wants to avoid labor problems. But what about the opposite situation? You know all about some area of the business that the new owners don't want any part of. If you're lucky, the whole business unit may be sold after the takeover or as part of the restructuring. For example, the Singer Company spun off its sewing machine division, the original and most famous part of the business, to the shareholders.

If you aren't lucky, and the new owners decide simply to dump the whole line, what do you do? You're very unlikely to be able to get away with lying, if you have a mind to, and say you don't do what you in fact do. Perhaps you might be able to look back into your resumé and point out your experience in an area in which the new owners are keenly interested. We'll look at an example of this in another chapter. But you also might be able to buy some time by selling the new owners on the virtue of what they don't want.

This happened when one huge aerospace company gobbled up another. The head of training at the acquired company was fired, and his training department was integrated into that of the parent company. This meant duplicate courses, and the head of training for the whole shebang, George, wanted to drop all the courses from the former training department of the acquired company.

Naturally, all the trainers there did not want to admit that their courses were lousy by comparison, nor were they eager to learn new courses that they didn't think were as good as the ones they themselves had developed. They called on their graduates, who peopled the acquired organization, to put in a good word for their training alma mater. The ploy worked. George took a year to eliminate and combine courses, which kept a lot of trainers on the payroll for an extra year while they looked around for new jobs.

As we've seen quite often in this book, the dominant company usually dictates to the dominated one what will be what. Often it just wipes up the floor with the bought company's managers. We've seen in the previous chapter that this may be due simply to a "cover your backside" mentality. If the new top brass fire a lot of people they then can cover their own incompetence by saying what a mess they found the company in when they took over. However, some psychologists have offered an alternative interpretation. They believe this overbearing domination is done out of fear by the perpetrators that they themselves will be dominated if they don't do it.

In any event you'd better make up your mind as fast as you can to accept the truth that the boss is the boss, even if he's the new boss, and you'd better keep your resumé in circulation. As David, who made out very well in the takeover of the California publishing house, says, "Either you adapt or you're gone." But getting back to our Robin Hood myth, how can you, a loyal Anglo Saxon, knuckle under to the "Norman dogs," as they're always called in the Robin Hood movies? A banker who also did just fine when his bank was taken over summed up his way of looking at it: "Is it any different from if you simply have a new boss, any new boss? Take the view, 'If I can make this guy look good, then this will help me in the long run.' Remember, there are people on both sides. The guy who has to come over to run your division has his problems too."

What Can You Expect If McKinsey Advises the Acquirer?

As we've noted, McKinsey has put the lie to the likelihood of putting together a successful business out of a successful takeover, especially a big one. This is no small statement, coming from such a distinguished firm, the one that produced, among other things, the research that went into *In Search of Excellence*.

What does McKinsey recommend to its clients? Obviously this will vary from job to job. However, there may be some general but useful answers in an interesting paper by a McKinsey partner, Steve Coley.

First of all, why all the bum mergers? Coley gives three general answers. One is overly optimistic market forecasts. An example was DuPont's acquisition of Conoco in the expectation of a boom in coal, which didn't happen. A second reason for the failures, according to Coley, is overestimating synergies. An example? "Phillip Morris's attempts to add consumer marketing muscle to 7-Up failed," cites the man from McKinsey. The third source of failure is lousy management of the acquisition. "Xerox's write-off of over $1 billion in its 1969 acquisition of SDS may be the largest, but Kennecott/Carborundum and Schlumberger/Fairchild are also notable post-acquisition failures," writes Coley, who adds, "Indeed an analysis of 18 recent acquisitions suggests that the performance of most of the acquired companies deteriorated significantly after the acquisition."

If these are the ways acquirers fail, how do they succeed, according to McKinsey? And, most important, suppose you as a manager are in a company taken over by a company advised by McKinsey, what can you expect? For openers, you should note that *your own* top management may have initiated the deal. "In fact," Coley notes, "investment bankers estimate that more than 80 percent of all transactions are seller initiated." Seller initiated? What about Icahn, Pickens, and the rest? They, by and large, are involved in the other 20 percent of the deals, although admittedly some big ones. But this is why they are outsiders. The deals McKinsey consults on are, to a great degree, the deals of Roundtable companies. So what we will see in the McKinsey analysis is the way the business establishment handles its takeovers. The ones that blow it do so by acting rashly, according to the McKinsey analysis. "Reactive responses to shopped companies, without benefit of in-depth analysis of either industry/company competitive economics or how the acquiree can create real value in the acquisition, leads to the majority of failed acquisition efforts," says Coley.

The paper notes that successful acquisitions are those in which at least two out of three "post-acquisition value adding levers" are employed. Here are the three:

1. Improving general management skills, for example, instilling an ROIC management philosophy and measurement system, tightening cost and working capital controls, or changing strategic direction. Back to William the Conqueror's number crunchers with their Doomsday Book.

2. Capturing functional synergies, for example, consolidating manufacturing, and transferring technology. Most of the successes here, according to Coley, were in the food industry, where the distribution, packaging, or advertising system of one company could be used to flog the products of the other.

3. Financial engineering, for example, "changing capital structures, stripping over-funded pension plans, spinning off assets to selected investor groups ... selling business units to alternate owners." This is precisely the bag of financial tricks used by the notorious corporate raiders, including the stripping of pension funds down to their legal minimums.

Now that we see what McKinsey advocates, we might want to see an example in practice. In this context, one whole paragraph in another McKinsey paper is so striking, it is worth quoting in its entirety:

"*Successful acquirers appear to apply a number of financial and operational levers to increase their probability of success.* In almost every successful acquisition in our sample, the acquiring firm was able to leverage its skills and assets to offset the acquisition premium, e.g., through operational expertise, general management skills, and financial engineering. Quaker's acquisition of Stokely Van Camp is an example. The acquisition was financed principally with debt, and Quaker was quick to divest many Stokely divisions where it could add little value. In addition, several unprofitable facilities were shut down, and redundant overheads eliminated. Stokely's remaining product lines were sold through Quaker's sales force who were active in expanding their geographic and demographic coverage. As a result, Stokely has been a very successful acquisition for Quaker. On the other hand, companies that relied exclusively on financial engineering, typically changing capital structure to finance an acquisition, were unsuccessful in almost every case."

Look what's happening here. Stokely was ground into oblivion, judging from this McKinsey paragraph. First of all, Quaker used debt to take it over. So what did they do about all that debt? The comparison to corporate raiders gets even more striking. The company was busted up, with some pieces sold off and others liquidated. Sounds like the raiders? Wait, there's more. Quaker flushed the Stokely staff jobs and showed no great respect for the "corporate culture" of the sales force either. And this is how the company that produced the research for *In Search of Excellence* sees things!

KEY POINTS

- The new corporate overseers may well be fast trackers making obscene amounts of money, often far more than was made by managers in the acquired company.

- Most of the new managers from corporate headquarters will be from finance and accounting—they really are number crunchers.

- Some managers can adapt quite well to the new management, prosper under it, and prefer the new ways to the old ways. And some of the "Norman Conquerors" are very decent people.

- There is no evidence that women are gaining because of the mergers. On the contrary, they must prove themselves all over again. The same holds true for minorities.

- Resentment is very common. The managers in the acquiring company tend to resent petty perks the acquired managers may hold onto. The managers in the acquired company resent their powerlessness, whether real or imaginary.

- You should accept the fact that the boss is the boss. Whether your company is taken over by Carl Icahn or by any Roundtable company that's advised by McKinsey, you probably won't be able to tell the difference.

4
THE FOURTH ORDEAL
Nothing Is Getting Done

The first three ordeals—the cascade of rumors, the torture over trying to figure out who will have power over you and what they'll be like, and the smoldering resentment between the old managers and the new ones, do not occur by themselves. They are accompanied by yet another element of chaos: Almost nobody's doing any work.

"During the period when our company was up for sale," said Greg, the CEO of an insurance company, "work slowed, diversion was coming upon our people, and some were fired when we saw it wasn't an environment that was suitable for them. A lot of people left."

A high-ranking member of the staff at the Continental Group reported a similar phenomenon. "As soon as Goldsmith made his offer, all the normal staff things came to a screeching halt," he said.

You have undoubtedly seen the phenomenon: As people panic and begin to fear that their new bosses are going to fire them no matter what they do, they stop doing nearly everything. The simplest things don't get accomplished. Phone calls aren't returned, and negotiations aren't completed—or if they are completed, the negotiated contracts aren't written up.

You've probably also seen the reasons for this. People aren't at their desks; they're in small rumor knots all over the office. Each boss is obsessing over his job and how he will protect "his people."

Also, the people who would routinely approve things stop doing it. Maybe they're waiting for new instructions. Maybe they're looking for new jobs. Maybe they've found them and are gone.

Recently, *The Wall Street Journal* ran an article on low morale at GM due to planned cuts of forty thousand white collar jobs. *Forty thousand?* The world's biggest industrial company doesn't mess around—it's cutting over one fourth of its people on salary. The article, by journalist Amal Kumar Naj, quotes a GM VP, Donald E. Hackworth: "We've got a lot of people sitting around wondering whether they'll be next. That's what gnaws on them." The article goes on to report:

> Some employees have become so consumed with who's leaving, and who might leave next, that they don't get much work done. "I spend a lot of time on the phone talking to guys who have been canned or guys who want to leave," says a quality control supervisor who confesses that his work has suffered. "I call them, they call me. GM has become a giant water cooler."

These cuts, of course, are all done in the name of competitiveness.

The Worker-Bee Approach

Greg, the CEO at the insurance company, who had worked his way to the top of his company during a series of takeovers, was not sympathetic to those who were part of the screeching halt at his company:

> It's unfair to the owner to sit around and fret. You're being paid, so to take their money and give them nothing for it is like theft. And it's also unfair to yourself, because no one is going to give you your day back.
>
> If you don't have the balls to put your resignation in, use the hiatus to clean the attic, do bypassed jobs—fixing weaknesses in control areas, for instance.
>
> I always took the attitude that so long as we're going down the same road together, let me take each decision on its own merits today, and if I do my part, I'll see what happens. I'm not going to listen to all the clatter. It's so important to cut it out. I haven't gotten anything out of the

clatter. I don't think in any extended way it's helpful. I had to form my own judgments. Do your own punch list.

Does this sound a bit like buttering up the bad guys? A little bit of identification with the aggressor? Maybe, but it worked. Greg went from middle management to top management, and then stayed there through several mergers. So his attitudes clearly fit the times.

But so can other attitudes. Barbara, the director of personnel at a major service company gobbled up by another, took the opposite position. "I think busywork is a foolhardy thing to force your subordinates to do. It flies in the face of human dignity and it's an insult," she said, adding:

> It lowers credibility and gets people cranky. Filling people with busywork in the name of earning an honest day's paycheck is simplistic because everyone wants to know at that point what's honest about the merger in the first place. Most people want to know that what they do counts, so the order to "look for something to do" may cause problems. I know of one department where a manager rebelled and did less and less.

However, there was an interesting little case study in this department. Everybody else in the department also did less and less, "except, for one person, who was a 'worker-bee,' a good little worker who will do whatever he's told to do," said Barbara. By the time the takeover was complete, the worker-bee was kept on and everyone else in the department was fired. So Barbara's attitude may have more dignity, but Greg's may be more likely to keep the paychecks coming in. Barbara, however, feels there's more to it. "The worker-bee was given more responsibility but no promotion. I know of other people who left who went on to better jobs," she said.

Along the worker-bee lines, New York management consultant Douglass T. Lind, who has consulted on the so-called integration phase of many mergers, urges that you "be perceived by others as well as by yourself as someone who gets on with the job by creating order out of chaos." For example, if someone walks, taking key information with him, you could throw up your hands in despair and join the rumor conspiracy, or you could take charge of putting the information back together. Lind urges that you go to your immediate boss and say, "Let me help you get moving." If it's the boss who has walked, go to your peers and say, "Let's get going."

This is most likely to be effective in areas where pivotal people have split—the systems department, development labs, the sales department. If the sales manager is the one who jumps ship, convene people and get their information pooled, urges Lind.

For example, a big metals company hammered several divisions together. Key sales people walked. Among those left was a man in his fifties, who took the lead in pooling the information. Previous to this he had had no one reporting to him. After helping to create order out of chaos, he backed off and went to his old job. "Who was that masked man?" asked top management admiringly of this Lone Ranger. They recognized that he was not a power grabber and decided that he would be helpful. He was in effect an empire builder who didn't keep the empire.

Doing Something Can Be Worse Than Doing Nothing

This is the good example, and both consultants and people who have been successful in such situations can report one or another version of it. But there's also the bad example. In one case, in a San Diego professional services firm, four managers, who were widely viewed as very effective, were suddenly on the outs as a result of a change of ownership. This caused work to slow in the company as people waited to see what would transpire.

One 35-year-old, who was making $60,000 a year, suddenly began to lobby the new management to bump the effective four. They were dumped, but afterwards he was perceived as a shill for the new bosses. He lost credibility with his peers and even with the new management, since his actions looked like a play for his own self-aggrandizement. Since he looked like an opportunist he was soon asked to seek his opportunities elsewhere.

So there is always a risk that doing something could be worse than doing nothing. "There are genuine issues of legitimate conflicting emotions," says San Francisco management consultant Jim Edgar of Edgar, Dunn and Conover, Inc. He continues:

> The key to being effective is to recognize that the conflicting emotions exist. This guy chose sides. The most effective kind of position to take is to say to yourself that you're going to handle your managerial responsibilities as effectively as you can and let this other stuff sort out as it has to. This is the right stance, both public and private.

This Marcus Aurelius posture is almost universally pushed by consultants and job counselors, and although it might be esthetically displeasing in the context of what the new owners inevitably seem to be up to, it also is advice that works—up to a point.

Playing a stoic Roman emperor may work only if somebody notices. If your boss and his boss skip or get booted out, who's going to know about your noble stand? Just because your boss is at his desk today doesn't mean he has a future there.

How Do You Combat Emotional Paralysis?

The other difficulty in taking the stoic position is that for many people it is emotionally impossible. They go into a depression as a consequence of feeling powerless. This saps their energy further and makes them even more ineffective at the job. However, according to a number of consultants, not everyone goes through the same cycle. According to consultant Lind, who is also a practicing psychoanalytic psychotherapist and a Presbyterian minister, there are two basic paths followed by people caught up in these ordeals.

"If the people are effective," says Lind, "they go into grief and work the problem through, but if they don't deal with it, confront it, they go into depression." This, he reports, is characterized by listlessness, lack of motivation, problems with eating and sleeping, and irrational outbursts of rage.

How do you get on the effective path? "You take some time to grieve," says Lind, "confront that fact, and then go into the chaos." An example was the stoic Lone Ranger.

According to a number of consultants, one way to stay on the effective path is to remember that you need the job. Since depression will work against your best interests, whatever might help prevent it can work to your benefit. This may involve doing something that seems slightly risky, such as speaking up, but because it will make you feel stronger, it can help to combat the depression.

There's often an opportunity to speak up because large groups of managers are typically brought together for official presentations about the changes. "In these big groups, managers generally don't ask questions out of fear of embarrassment, looking stupid, or looking disloyal," says Denver consultant Richard C. Ten Eyck, who consulted on a change in strategic direction that would involve retrenchment at a large hospital with over 2,000 employees. "All of these fears of asking questions are baloney," he asserts. He advises that six or seven managers get together before the meetings and write down half a dozen key questions, including the big one: What about my job and security?

"This gets the topic on the table, allows the middle managers to unload their concern, and by acting as a group prevents anyone from being singled out," says Ten Eyck. What if top management singles out the whole group and fires the lot? "They might," says Ten Eyck, acknowledging that this is the risk. But he claims the argument for doing it may outweigh the risk:

> It becomes spoken instead of unspoken and therefore doesn't eat away at you. [If you let these concerns eat away, they make] you less productive, or totally nonproductive, to the point where it becomes evident to top management that you should be a candidate for dismissal because you can't adjust.

Beating the emotional paralysis seems to be the key to making a good impression on the new management, since this allows you to work more hours. According to Ten Eyck, "The guy who puts in 60 hours is really going to shine in this situation, unless he's a klutz, since the new management and the new owners are looking for people who are willing to make a sacrifice and not skimp on time."

What if the company takes all your time and still kicks you out into the street? "[Working long hours] is still no guarantee that you won't get sacrificed," adds consultant Ten Eyck.

Motivating the Troops

Despite the risk that they may be wasting their time, many managers want to get revved up so they can put in their extra hours. So motivational training is making a big comeback. For years most companies were only interested in measurable skills training. With this type of training, you give a test beforehand, then the training program, then a test afterwards, and see whether or not the person learned something—such as how to do well on a test.

But with widespread demoralization, more and more companies have been hiring motivational trainers. Here the ability to measure whether anyone has learned anything is questionable. Ron Zemke, senior editor of *Training* magazine, calls this sort of touchy-feely stuff, "woo woo" training. The ultimate example is fire walking, where people walk barefoot over burning coals while they imagine they are stepping gingerly over cool, wet moss.

One of the biggest of the motivational training programs of the early '70s was est, Erhard Seminars Training, which put together diverse elements from Dale Carnegie, Zen, Scientology, and elsewhere to produce a highly controversial two-weekend course in personal motivation. About half a million people paid $300 each to go through it. The man who developed it, Werner Erhard, has now developed a motivational training for business in which he promises "breakthroughs" based on "transformations" of the organization. "We essentially try to get clients to go to the office with the intention of sticking their necks out instead of covering their asses," says one person affiliated with the organization.

Not everyone believes that quick change is possible in organizations. Tom Peters, co-author of *In Search of Excellence*, has said:

> The possibility of est transforming corporate America is zero. The possibility of Tom Peters transforming corporate America is zero. Anybody who helps an organization come to grips with change is my friend, but anybody who promises to dramatically change anything—particularly someone else's organization—is either a jerk or an egomaniac.

What happens if you feel great about the takeover, but those under you don't? How do you get them fired up? One time-honored solution has already been mentioned by Greg, the CEO of the insurance company. You could fire a few of them to get the message across to the rest. However, this army-of-occupation solution can work against you too, creating additional resentment, and additional sudden departures, just when you don't want them.

"You should try not to go in as the macho manager," says Barbara, the director of personnel quoted earlier. "People *know* there's no reason to go back to work," she says, adding,

> If you go in as a manager who wants to portray business as usual, people aren't fools, they know it's not business as usual. So it's a bad idea to come in and pump the corporate pipeline, saying "Let's go ahead, nothing has changed." On the contrary, there's a need to acknowledge that things have changed. The string of pearls has broken and the pearls have fallen on the floor. Your job is to restring them. Maybe you won't find all of them, and maybe you won't put them back in the same order, but you can still make a beautiful necklace.

Macho managing can create not only open resistance but also passive resistance. You may not even know that someone is quietly holding up a key part of the work. Then one day the passive resister splits and you're left holding the bag for a job undone. How was

Greg able to get away with it? He was shrinking the business by 50 percent, which meant he was significantly overstaffed. Under these circumstances, the exceedingly hardnosed solution worked. It might even qualify, under the circumstances, as leadership.

However, most definitions of leadership advocate enlisting the help of those who work under you. So what do you do to motivate them and at the same time avoid scaring anyone off?

Merger consultant Price Pritchett urges top management to follow a series of steps to deal with these problems. Even if you're not one of the Big Boys, some of his points might be useful to you in dealing with your own subordinates.

Keep People Informed

As his number one point, Pritchett urges top management to "explain the reasons for the change." As we have seen, top management often can't or doesn't want to do this. But insofar as possible, see if you can figure out what the reasons for the takeover or retrenchment are, and communicate them to your subordinates. We've seen that many people already assume that top management is lying to them. If they figure you are too, then you're through as far as getting real cooperation goes. So don't lie unless you're prepared to pay the consequences.

This is one topic on which nearly everyone seems to agree. "Keep people terribly, terribly informed, at the risk of being overly informed," says Barbara, the director of personnel. She adds,

> If you don't know what's going on, tell them that. You can tell them something one day, and change it the next if you say something like, "Here's what I thought yesterday, this is what I found out today." My boss did that, and I give him credit for it. Before the merger, he would routinely inflate the information he knew, but during the turmoil, there were many times that he didn't know and he said it. Everyone respected him for it. There's more power in telling the truth than in someone finding out that you didn't know but pretended that you did.

In communicating with the people who report to you about the change that is taking place, there are a few guidelines most consultants recommend.

First, don't ad lib. Find out what you can and figure out the best way to explain it to people. Also, tell them more than once, just to make sure they get it. Second, you may find it unwise to endorse the takeover because you could be viewed as a traitor by everyone who works for you. However, even if you don't endorse the new setup, you should point out and talk up its possible advantages and opportunities for the people who work for you. Everyone's likely to be knocking it, but you get nowhere by knocking it too. If you don't see any hope in it, why should anyone who works for you, and then, why should they work hard? Third, figure out specifically what each person who works for you can do to integrate into the new setup, and tell each one personally. As part of this, ask each one specifically and personally for help. If they aren't loyal to the organization anymore, maybe they'll be loyal to you.

Fourth, tell people it will be tough and there will be problems; you want them to have a mental set to expect problems and be willing to deal with them.

Get People Involved

Another key step urged by Pritchett is to "arrange for participation and involvement." This is something you should certainly try to do. Get the ideas of everyone who works under you. You may be surprised at the wisdom you'll find. Alice, a human resources executive at a large consumer goods company being taken over, found out in this way that her new secretary had been through several previous mergers at other companies. "She could see through the memos coming from headquarters better than I could," said Alice, "and this helped me to prepare for the flood of people who came to my office." One way to get participation is to hold lots of meetings to minimize the sense of isolation. The assumption of managers who choose the path of busywork for their subordinates is that the busier your subordinates appear to be in a chaotic office, the better the chance that you will stand out as their manager and be kept on, which increases the odds for those doing the busywork—the people who work for you. If you do go the busywork route, talk to each person about specific projects he or she might want to work on and set specific target dates for their completion.

Provide Direction

Pritchett, and many other consultants, urge a strong display of leadership. What does this mean for a middle manager caught up in the merger? One big element is visibility. Be there. Make sure your subordinates see you. Keep your office door open, wander around, call them in—whatever it takes to make them aware of your presence. Leadership also means giving clear direction. If you're using the busywork approach, and your subordinates don't seem to know what they should be doing, you should. This could be a time for at least a six month plan for your part of the business, and you could get ideas on this from your subordinates.

What in the world would you do with a plan at a time like this? Pitch it to the new man who will undoubtedly be arriving from corporate and whom you should try to get access to (See "The Second Ordeal: Who Are These Guys?"). Based on the plan, ask yourself, "If I were the owner looking at my piece of this business, what would I expect out of my job?"

Minneapolis consultant Stephen Faunce suggests that you boil down the pitch to three 10-minute segments:

> Take the first 10 minutes to explain what can be done functionally without further approval. Then give 10 minutes to what you consider to be opportunities in this area—down-to-earth, not blue-sky, ideas, based on a new owner with deep pockets. Explain the needed investment and the payback for it, and how the organization will be better off after than before and by how much. For the third 10 minutes, lay out the most significant problems and what's being done or could be done to deal with them.

All of this would be enhanced if you had a plan to wave around. Will it all be futile if this hard-boiled egg plans to roll over you anyway? Sure, but at least you tried. If he wants to be a fool and fire an effective leader who kept his head when everyone around him was going crazy, that's his problem.

If you don't believe in busywork, what does clear direction mean? First, go over all the work that your department routinely does and decide which is critical for the survival of the organization. Then make sure this core piece of the work gets done. Subordinates will be hard-pressed to argue that this is futile. In most cases, essential work comes back at you fast if it's not done on time or correctly. "If the payroll stops functioning, you'll hear about it fast," says Barbara, the personnel director. Second, with the remaining time, get people to focus on themselves in a constructive way. Tell them to get on the phone and start looking for another job. But use discretion, your own boss may not want you to do this. Try to get people to avoid dwelling on the resentment. Advises Barbara, "It's a waste of energy to think about the top brass. People will kill time focusing on how big someone's parachute is when they could be on the phone finding out about the next course at the local community college which could help them."

Calm the Clients

If the employees are in choas over the takeover, what about the customers or clients? They're often wondering whether or not they should stick with your company. In fact, they're not even sure what your company is anymore. So one thing you can do if you are in touch with the clients is to go out and calm them down. But what do you say? "The key," says Ward Naughton, of Edgar, Dunn & Conover of San Francisco, "is that you're out there. Even if you don't have all the information, you have to make them feel they will be the most important user of that information once you get it."

For example, after one big bank gobbled up another, a Fortune 500 client of the eaten bank got worried. How would their cash management services be transferred to the new institution? Naughton, who was with the taken-over bank at the time, put together a formal review of what the client had with his old bank and assured the customer that this would be supplied to the acquirer once it was formally in charge. "This helped to reassure them," reports Naughton.

KEY POINTS

- When the work bogs down, gain a reputation as someone who gets on with the job by creating order out of chaos.

- If someone walks away taking key information with him, don't throw up your hands in despair, but take charge of putting the information back together.

- On the other hand, evaluate each activity or project separately; be aware when doing something *is* worse than doing nothing.

- Take some time to grieve and confront feelings of powerlessness. You'll be more effective if you admit to these feelings than if you let them smolder.

- Beat emotional paralysis by posing smart questions to the new management.

- To make sure your subordinates remain effective, be honest with them, acknowledge the changes, and keep them informed on a regular basis.

THE FIFTH ORDEAL
The Scramble To Fit In

The first four ordeals of the takeover involve rumors, confusion, taking sides, and chaos. Although they provoke more anxiety than anyone needs, they are driven largely by real, often visible, external forces. There really *are* rumors. The new managers *are* a mystery. People *are* taking sides. Things *are* in chaos.

The fifth ordeal is far more sinister. It strikes you from the inside, gnawing at your self-confidence just at the moment when you need it most, and thus weakening your ability to handle all the other problems. Like a fifth column, the fifth ordeal subverts your strength.

Until the takeover, you may have believed that you fit in very well. But all of a sudden the way things are done has changed, the bosses have changed, the organizational structure has changed or is very likely to do so. You were well adapted to the old set-up, so your fear is: What do the new guys need you for?

What Questions Will Top Management Ask?

They fall into two general categories: the luck questions and the opportunity questions. Even though you cannot influence the answers, you'd be very foolish to ignore the luck questions, since they are a giveaway as to whether or not you're trying for something you can't get, no matter what you do.

Questions of Luck

We'll start with the questions of luck. They generally cover three areas: economics, age, and the new owners' attitude toward middle managers.

Economics. "This, for me, is a repeat play of what I saw in New England in my teens during the late forties," says James E. Barrett, 57, managing director of Cresheim Management Consultants, Philadelphia. "Managers thought they were losing their jobs because of a postwar recession, but really it was because the textile industry was moving South," he continues. "Few of those laid-off people ever worked again at the work for which they were qualified. What paid the bills was the same thing as now—working wives and social programs," he says. So the economic question is simply this: *Is top management making a fundamental business change that doesn't include you?*

Age. Barrett urges those trying to decide whether they can fit in to ask themselves the second key question: *How old are you?* He elaborates: "If you have general managers in their fifties and sixties, then, for the organization's dynamics, the rank behind them should be in their forties. This means all of the others in their late forties and early fifties who would be eligible for better jobs are potentially surplus, unless there's some other reason to keep them."

Harsh? Worse than that, it's appalling. Legal? Absolutely not; in fact these age-based firings are a crass violation of federal law. But they're a fact. Just look at any outplacement office. "A sea of gray hair," is how New York outplacement consultant Jay Bushell has described the situation.

Attitude Toward Middle Management. The third question concerns the "make or buy" decision. Many people in law, training, public relations, and other fields could be cut from the staff and the services bought from an outside vendor. Incidentally, and not surprisingly, the outside vendors who are always recommending that the company buy from outside vendors.

Then, the company might be viewing you simply as a current expense, with no payback that shows on the books. Many middle managers in R&D or market development show up in these categories. According to Barrett, the traditional cost of a typical middle manager including salary, benefits, memberships, cost of office space, telephones, and support programs comes to $125,000. By getting rid of the middle manager and his job slot, the company gets rid of this expense.

However, some top executives think the $125,000 figure greatly underestimates the true expense of a middle manager. It assumes that he or she is just sitting around waiting for orders to fall from above so they can be sent on to subordinates below. In fact, so this argument goes, many middle managers are dynamic and scheme up projects to justify their jobs. Since these programs also cost, the true savings in axing a middle manager may be as much as $500,000. But are these projects valuable to the company? "The true test," according to Barrett "is whether the projects disappear when the middle manager does, or a year or two later." For some reason, if the projects do fall away, then they presumably were worthless. Of course, this is like saying that when Albert Einstein left the Swiss patent office, he took something completely valueless with him—the theory of relativity.

Keys to Survival

So much for the questions concerning luck. Now for the good news, the questions top management will ask that will afford you opportunities. We'll look at actual cases where managers have prospered during takeovers, show how they did it, and raise the key questions the new management would ask in these situations.

Having a recognized track record. "I managed through three takeovers, and in each case I was in the target," says Seth, the 60-year-old chief financial officer of a small New England lingerie manufacturing company. He had not only survived, but prospered. Some people do in these ordeals, and this man's story illustrates several of the key ways.

Seth hadn't always been on top of things. He had simply been a cost accountant at a Boston candy manufacturer and retailer. But as part of his job there, he had taken on the responsibility of designing and installing new computer systems for the company. Then came the takeover.

"The new company needed someone who could do this sort of thing for them," says Seth. But how did the new owners know about this little cost accountant? "At the candy company, I had reported directly to the president. I was highly visible, and he must have put in a good word for me to the new owners" Seth reports. "I was the only one transferred over to the new company, which sent me to

IBM to take a course in data processing." So not only was he singled out for special treatment, but the new owners immediately started to invest in him. All the evidence was that they intended to keep him and that he would prosper under the new set-up.

There's a key survival issue which this success story already illustrates. Seth had a recognized track record at the company taken over. Most search firms, management consultants, and outplacement consultants stress the importance of this issue. For example, Calvin K. Sholl, CEO of the search firm Parker, Sholl, and Gordon, Inc., of Boston, is quite emphatic on this point. "Of compelling importance is performance as measured by productivity and track record under the former ownership." Seth makes the same point. "The advice I'd give to middle managers," he says, "is to ask themselves, 'Do I have a track record behind me?' If you don't, get the hell out in a hurry. Better to get another job while you still have one. But if you have a good track record behind you, they'll compare yours with their guy's." And if you look good, you might, like Seth, get transferred over to join him, or even replace him.

In other words, to be successful with the new owners, you may well have had to be successful with the old owners.

Being indispensable. Five years later, Seth was manager of systems and data processing at his company. He didn't waste these years collecting a paycheck and telling everyone how great he was. Instead, he innovated in a unique way. "I designed and installed an inventory control system, that accomplished more than IBM's system could." It also did something else, which may well be the most important single thing one can do to survive in a merger.

"The ones who survive are indispensable in one way or another," says management consultant Douglass T. Lind of the Trisource Group, Westport, Connecticut, and a man who has consulted on the consolidation phase of many mergers, including some huge ones. "They can't be replaced," he continues, "because of a scarcity of their talent in the marketplace, a unique understanding of the technology, or even because the person who replaced them would have too steep a learning curve." What about someone like Seth, the systems manager? "It's very common that the systems man is kept," says Lind, "because he has unique knowledge." Notice that Seth, the systems man, had developed his own system. He knew how it worked and how to fix it if it didn't. A replacement might not have known these matters as well.

Systems people aren't the only ones who are indispensable. Sales people with special ties to the customers, accountants who know where the bodies are buried, and secretaries who know where the papers are filed may all fit into the same indispensability niche. So can operations people who jerry-rig the machinery. An example happened in one mining, smelting, and refining company that was acquired by another. The 50-year-old man in the target company who was running the smelter was kept because the technology was too specialized to replace him. He had held the operation together with spit and chewing gum during a time when it had been starved for cash, and now his innovation had saved his job; the new owners were afraid no one else could keep the refinery running.

There are other types of hard core indispensability. Top management may ask, Would getting rid of this person devastate the organization? Would he take 50 other people with him?

For example, a 43-year-old general sales manager in an electronics manufacturing firm had the loyalty of the sales force, and he was in a strong industry position as well. He was well known from participating on a key electrical industry association committee that set standards for certain commercial products. This, in turn, helped to make him a frequently invited speaker and resulted in various co-authored papers. So he had a network which he had set up for good business reasons, but which he could at any moment use for survival reasons. He could get another job, and he might take some others with him.

Although these types of indispensability are real, a fully indispensable person should not be shocked if he gets booted out anyway. How could that happen? Not everyone among the new top management puts the stockholders' interests first. In trying to figure out how the top people view you, keep in mind one fact. The departure of anybody in a large corporation always represents an opportunity for a lot of people because it puts things in flux. "In a large corporation, they are rarely sorry to lose anyone," says consultant Barrett. Even if a person has hard core, economic indispensability, his departure may be viewed as an opportunity by many people in the organization. Therefore, although the second key survival technique is to make yourself indispensable to the new owners because without you they will surely lose money, it still may not work.

How can those making the "keep or fire" decisions justify dumping an indispensable person? Easy. All they have to do is put doubt in the minds of their own bosses about the prospects of keeping the indispensable person even if they offer that person a place. This is easy to do, because they already know, even if they haven't said, how nasty the work environment will be while they struggle to pay off the huge debt taken on in the takeover. Many in the new top management may be wondering in their heart of hearts why anyone would be crazy enough to want to stay. This is more or less the reverse of Groucho Marx's line that he wouldn't consider joining any club that would have him as a member. The sorts of issues the new executive who may be maneuvering to bump an indispensable person will look at are the person's marketability, family issues, kids in school, outside interests tying him to the locale, and whether in private moments he has expressed dissatisfaction with the company to people he had mistakenly thought he could trust.

In addition to economic indispensability, there's a softer kind, which is not economic, but psychological. It will not operate in all takeovers because it depends entirely on its being recognized by key people, and they themselves may not survive the merger. However, this other kind of indispensability is worth noting since it extends the concept beyond the limited circle of those who are economically indispensable. The strategies that lead to psychological indispensability are essentially the same as those of being a good subordinate. They have been noted in a book by Jeffrey P. Davidson, *Blow Your Own Horn*.

One strategy is always to make the boss look good. Why should a boss part with someone who makes him look good and risk replacing him with someone who might make him look bad? Notice that this strategy would be useless if your boss jumps ship, which he might be in a position to do since you have made him look good to headhunters.

A second strategy is to give credit away, to the boss, to subordinates, and to the group. One senior VP at a major entertainment conglomerate, who survived several restructurings at his company, said, "If you give away credit which is due you, everyone notices and immediately assumes that you are the sort of person that they want to have around—someone who gets things done but doesn't threaten anyone. Higher ups want you to work for them, since they figure they don't have to keep looking over their shoulder at you; their back is covered." Again, this only helps if the higher ups who have noticed have also survived.

A third strategy is to take on the unwanted jobs. An example is organizing the Christmas party or even the dinners for the merger. The showbiz VP explained, "Nobody wanted to do this, because if it was lousy, everyone would notice. One trick, if it's a sit-down dinner party, is to give yourself the worst seat, and also the one nearest the service door. That way, if anyone complains you can always say, 'Yeah, did you see where I was sitting?'"

A fourth strategy is simply to praise the boss. Be careful with this one, since you mustn't be an obvious apple polisher. People who have reached any significant level in large companies are usually pretty smart and they know when they're being flattered. But they also may be insecure and could use the emotional support, so when they do something right, let them know about it. Again, this strategy is useless if you've buttered up a guy who gets fired or splits for a better job without taking you along.

Getting noticed. But how do you know whether the top people view you favorably? One thing to look for is whether or not they put you on the appropriate consolidation committees. "I was put on a committee of counterparts with all other companies they had acquired," says Seth, the indispensable systems man. He was also promoted within his own taken-over company. His new job was director of information systems and controller. "If you sense that you're not included in key consolidating meetings where they'll get the benefit of the acquisition by eliminating some people," Seth advises, "then figure that they've decided to get rid of you. If you're not on those committees, then get out while you still have a job, while you still look like a successful person."

So the third key to survival, in addition to a proven track record and indispensability, is to make sure you're on the consolidation committees. If you're not but you should be, then that's a tip-off that you may be marked for elimination. But how do you get on these committees if your track record isn't so hot and you aren't indispensable? One way, if you want to do it, is to become indispensable by playing politics.

This is what Elliot, the 42-year-old head of all staff positions in the major group of a manufacturing corporation did. The company, composed of three groups, was reeling from a recent greenmail shakedown and so was implementing a downsizing. As we've seen repeatedly in this book, staff jobs are usually the first to go. But this didn't happen in Elliot's case. He and all of his top subordinates survived. The same can't be said for ten division presidents who reported to our staff-man's boss, the group executive. Within a few months, four were gone, four were demoted, and only two made it to new division presidencies.

How had this happened? Elliot played on the insecurities of the group executive, making himself the eyes and ears of this gentleman, and convincing him he couldn't trust the other division presidents. He managed to get himself put in charge of the reorganization, controlling access to the group executive and becoming the trusted idea man to the boss. The group executive had come out of operations, and felt insecure about marketing and strategic thinking. Elliot was perfectly prepared to give him confidence. Naturally his own staff department had to take some cuts too. Five hundred jobs were axed. Most were in the $20,000 to $30,000 range. Those who were paid $100,000 to $150,000 were kept. Elliot defined the reality for the group executive and was able to sell him on this type of cut.

Politics can chase a lot of talent out of companies. For example, after three years, Seth, the indispensable, highly visible systems man with a track record who was the controller at his company, decided to jump ship for a Boston frozen foods company. The food company needed his talent to update their computer systems. But the old company, which had made him controller, was shocked. "They were amazed since I was making good money," he reports.

At his new employer, he again made himself indispensable. "I put in a cost center accounting system, which separated out where we were making money and where not. I also put in an innovative warehousing system." Of course, his indispensability needed rewards or he'd leave, so the company promoted him to the number two position. "I knew how to price the product," he reports, adding, "They needed me."

However, there was a good deal of consolidation going on in the food processing industry at this time, and his new company got caught up in it. A Canadian fish processing company swallowed it up, and then an even bigger fish company ate the first one. Seth, the innovator, ran into politics. "They were overloaded with management, had lots of politics, and thought their systems were better than mine. I knew I couldn't win the politics—they're Canadian and I'm American. They kept *saying* they'd keep me, but I sensed they wouldn't. So I switched jobs while I still had one."

This is when he became the CFO of the lingerie manufacturing company.

> I went to all my friends around here. The bankers knew me, and when a CFO passed away the CEO got in touch with me through a placement agency. What attracts management is someone who can find problems, define them in simple terms, and then solve them. Now I'm the VP of finance and administration, and I've turned this company from a moderately profitable to a highly profitable one. I've done the same thing now about six times. Each time I found I only had to use my same basic knowledge. Each time it's been easier. I brought innovation and crea-

tivity into each of these businesses. I was always a little ahead of the game.

Notice the basic lessons of this man who has succeeded both because of and in spite of takeovers: First, he established a track record, which was highly visible. Second, he made himself indispensable. Third, he kept his eyes open and got out of highly charged political situations where people who based their success on merit might get caught out. In other words he always operated where his strengths would get rewarded.

Luck or Flexible Attitude?

"No question I lucked out," says Jack, who is the CEO of a Texas financial services company that had been sold and resold several times over the past few years. "I'm still dodging the bullet by having amicable owners," says the 47-year-old executive, adding, "Also, I'm getting trained—there's something that goes with doing something several times. You don't control a damned thing but you get plugged into how things work and what to expect."

His experiences show that he had, for a while, two kinds of luck—having the right buyers and being in the right industry. But he also had the right set of attitudes to go with the luck, so he could take full advantage of it by seeing his opportunities. He needed those attitudes, because his luck didn't hold. His story illustrates another quality of survivors noted by a number of consultants—flexibility.

In the mid-seventies the financial services company's parent company went into Chapter 11, and a large bank took ownership of the very successful financial services company in lieu of payment of debt by the bankrupt parent company. From a manager's standpoint, this was a lucky break, since the bank was legally required to dispose of the financial services company within two years. This was no fire sale; they took all of the two years to do it, hiring a major Wall Street investment banking house to find a buyer. During this time the owner-bank practically begged the financial services company management to stay on since they needed continuity of management to make the deal.

The luck continued when the Wall Street firm sent a mid-level nonpartner to work on the sale. "He came to us and asked us to feed him information and get the story told straight," says Jack, who was then a middle-level executive in the finance area of the financial services company, adding, "We could even do a modest amount of self-advertising."

This led to his next bit of luck. The buyer turned out to be a huge conglomerate that was interested in expanding the financial services business but didn't know anything about it. So they, too, begged everyone in management to stay. However, one man left, and Jack, then a middle manager, suddenly was made senior VP of finance. "The new owner had access to capital and was supportive in modestly building the business," he says. Up to this point Jack's attitude was helpful; he recognized opportunities that were in front of him, but it wasn't hard to do so because he was in a lucky situation.

Then the luck started to run out, and this is when Jack's attitude began to play a pivotal role. The parent company hired a major consulting firm to do an analysis of all of their subsidiaries. They pigeonholed them into four squares—dogs to be liquidated, cash cows to be milked, stars to be promoted, and question marks to play Hamlet over. The financial services company had the bad luck to land in the question mark square. This was because the Federal Reserve Bank had just raised interest rates and this end of the financial services industry was not so obviously good anymore. "They decided to put my company up for sale," he says, "since we required cash to grow, but the market was pretty good for companies like ours and they sold it for two and a half times what they paid."

Jack was personally involved as the number two man in the selling effort. "So all the prospective buyers got to know me from the beginning," he recalls. This, of course, is what every manager hopes will happen in a takeover, but it also was filled with booby traps. He recalls the dilemma: "You wanted to see your company sold, but you didn't want to overrepresent things, because you hoped you'd be on the other side and then you'd have to be accountable for what you said." This was something like a used Rolls Royce salesman hoping he'd then be hired on as the chauffeur. This presented a conflict of loyalties, which is worth noting:

> It was really important to say to ourselves collectively that we had an obligation to our present owners to do our best for them, regardless of what was on the other side for us. It was really a fundamental ethical question. You got caught up in so many representations that you really couldn't say things that you couldn't say to both buyer and seller in the same room at the same time, even if one party didn't like it. Otherwise you'd be a whore for one side or the other.

The Scramble To Fit In

This attitude seems to be characteristic of many who succeed in these takeovers. They simply stick with the truth of the situation and don't try to second guess it or shade it with hopes or fears. Of course, Jack was in a unique position to do this since he was as close to the deal as it was possible to be. Nonetheless, he still did not know what the new owners *really* had in mind.

One management consultant, James M. Edgar of Edgar, Dunn & Conover, of San Francisco, recommends this strategy for those who are lucky enough to have maximum information. "Be patient," advises Edgar, "It will become obvious, and the initial behavior you see may give a wrong impression. It takes time—6, 12, or 18 months for the full impact of the acquiring company to set in."

Jack needed a lot of patience. His financial services company was bought by another conglomerate, which had been expanding in the financial services area. However, this particular purchase was rammed down the throats of the financial services executives by top management, who, in spending $90 million, closed out a lot of other deals that the financial services people had cooking. "So we started out as mildly resented by the financial services executives," recalls Jack.

However, despite the potential politics, he still had the luck of the draw. "In this industry at the time, people weren't being fired," he recalls.

But the parent did fire someone—Jack's boss. Consultant Jim Edgar has an interesting observation on this sort of thing. "After the acquisition, some of the things you don't like about the old organization may improve—someone who wasn't in the old guard may get a chance after the acquisition."

Jack got his chance—sort of. Because the conglomerate couldn't make any decisions, they couldn't decide on whom to put in the top slot. So Jack was made co-head of his financial services company along with the head of marketing. "We agreed to agree," he recalls, adding, "And while we did this, the competition was kicking our brains out. It was hard to reach anything that looked like a tough decision. It was a classic example of how not to run a company."

During this time the big question was who would become the new president of his financial services company—the marketing man or Jack? Neither got it. An outsider was brought in, and Jack was effectively demoted to executive VP of finance. To survive with his luck down, he needed an attitude that was up, and he had it:

> I took the attitude, "Look, I'm still working for this company; I've seen people come and go. This guy may be the

right one, let's give it a shot." So I made up my mind to rally in the face of people saying, "You didn't get the job, do you want to go back to your old job?" For a lot of years I've felt I had a one-day relationship with this company. I felt I was providing value to the company so I figured they'd know that. Trouble was, the new boss had a strained relationship with virtually everyone. But I've seen people not get along with their bosses, leave, and then not get along with three more bosses. I've felt very strongly that a fair amount of flexibility was required of me.

Then the conglomerate was raided. It turned to a White Knight that ultimately busted it up. Jack's financial services company was sold again, ending up in the hands of people who took a different direction. "The strategic direction of the company is in a quasi-liquidating mode, to make assets available to service the debt they took on to buy the company," points out Jack, who was promoted to president and put in charge of this new direction. Jack is a lucky survivor with the right attitude for seeing opportunities. He has cut the company's payroll by 50 percent. "Pruning it back so it can come back to life, there may be redeployment, maybe in another business," he says.

Jack, the CEO, sums up this bizarre tale of survival based on luck and attitude:

> Each one of these things has its own dynamic; you grow. Each is almost like changing jobs—new skill requirements, opportunity to look at and implement new strategies, new sets of owners, a chance to prove yourself over again. It's been dynamic. I'm more anxious than five, six years ago, but you've got to grit it out somewhere. It's better than sitting around with half a day on my hands. Today is simply another punch list. I don't have the stress because I'm not sure this isn't the way things are.

The lesson here is that if you are lucky you'll be provided with opportunities. If you're flexible, you'll be able to take advantage of them, fit in, and maybe even prosper.

Another example of this is Harry, age 45, making $70,000 a year as a manager in the R&D labs of a Fortune 500 electronics company when it was taken over by another company in the same industry. His job was not immediately threatened. On the contrary, he was needed to help the company shift its product research direction.

Previously the company had done a considerable amount of basic research and also research leading to the introduction of totally new, innovative products. However, the new owners had taken on a lot of debt to buy Harry's company, and they immediately dropped all basic research and much R&D leading to the introduction of new products. Instead, the new direction called for ways to repackage and recycle existing products to make the fastest buck possible.

Harry was not amused. He did not like the new direction, and he especially didn't like directing scientists into efforts that he thought were unworthy of their talents. However, he also had a big investment in this company, having spent 15 years there, ultimately moving up to management positions from the technical jobs where he had started. "I felt stuck," he reported, adding, "I had never thought about my career, I just had gotten where I was by working hard."

Flexibility saved him. He suddenly realized the significance of being in a two-track company. One track was managerial, which was where he was at that time. The other track was scientific/technical, which was where he had started. He resolved his problem by switching back to the scientific track. The company wisely let him do this, realizing that it didn't want to lose a valuable person, so his switch was made without penalty. But was he out of touch with scientific innovation? No, because he had not been so senior in management that this was a problem.

Harry's switch to technical work is the reverse of what has been happening in Houston with the decline in the oil industry. Many geologists and technical people have been thrown out of work there. Some join Forty Plus, a nonprofit outplacement club for managers and technical people over age 40. They help each other to find work. Unlike in many Forty Plus offices, one person, Mrs. Pat Slater, is on salary there as the executive director. She has seen quite a few scientists switch to sales jobs and, to their surprise, like it. "They came in thinking there's only one area they really fit, and then new opportunities come up, and they say, 'you couldn't drag me back to the old job,'" she reports.

How About Fitting in By Relocating?

Sometimes the flexibility required to hang onto the job after the takeover is more than a mere change in attitude, which is wrenching enough for most people. Sometimes, if you want to stay with the company, you have to physically move. Not everyone is willing to do it. For example, Sam, 50, was the national sales manager for a division of a major California consumer products company. Due to problems in another division, the company was a sitting duck for raiders, who made a run on it. They were successfully fought off, but in a resultant cost-cutting measure, the entire outside selling organization was eliminated, with the company switching to telephone sales. Sam's job was zapped. However, he was offered an alternative to the street. If he wanted to relocate from San Francisco to a small town in North Carolina to take a job with different title and responsibilities but the same money, he could stay with the company. Here's how Sam explained his decision to take early retirement:

> I decided not to move to the boondock town. I had been with this firm for 27 years and had been in this town for 25 years. The issues of family and friends transcended the job. Also I just didn't want to move to that other place; I had been there before. Even though my kids were out of the house and even out of school, I just didn't want it. Besides, with 26 years of profit sharing, my severance package was reasonable.

Sam, of course, could comfortably turn down the move. But even those who are not so well situated frequently turn down job relocations for reasons such as having kids in school, their spouse's holding a good job where they are, or the general uncertainty of the business world—Why introduce more into one's life by relocating? Brian Moran, of Moran, Stahl, and Boyer, Inc., a consulting firm that specializes in helping companies move, thinks this reluctance to move does not help one's career prospects. He explains:

> You should accept the idea of movement because as soon as the ink is dry on the takeover, the technology, organization, and products of the company are already obsolete and can change instantly. Getting a mindset which is negative to movement is not advantageous from a career standpoint. Besides, if you turn down the move, you might find the next job requires a move anyway.

Moran's company has done extensive research on the various factors that indicate whether a move will lead to success or disaster. They've done it for both foreign and domestic moves, but since joining the corporate foreign legion may seem too drastic a way to survive a takeover, we'll focus here only on their results for domestic moves. Here are some of the items on their list:

1. *Career perspective.* If you figure the move fits into what you were planning anyway, you'll have an easier time succeeding at it than you would otherwise.

2. *Future job expectations.* If you have positive expectations, your attitudes are much more likely to lead to success than negative ones would. But if you're too happy-go-lucky, and don't have a realistic view of the challenges, you may not succeed.

3. *Job communications.* How can you keep them down on the farm once they've seen the farm? If you think you've been misled, or not led at all about what things will be like, your chances for success may not be so great.

4. *Job/company satisfaction.* If you're not keen on the company because of the takeover, you'll be taking that attitude with you to the new place, and it won't help matters.

5. *Choice.* If you feel your choices are either to move to the new location or move into the outplacement office, your likelihood for success is diminished compared to those who had lots of real choices.

6. *Area expectations.* If you don't like the new area, watch out.

7. *Community involvement.* People who become actively involved in the community tend to do well on moves.

8. *Extended family importance.* If you liked being close to your parents, aunts, uncles, and cousins before the move, but can't be because of lack of proximity afterwards, you may be in trouble. On the other hand, if you don't particularly like your extended family, the move could be the opportunity of a lifetime.

9. *Ability to cope with failure.* If you can bounce back, you may travel well.

10. *Humor.* If you can laugh the demons of frustration and difficulty in the face, you're beginning to look like a shoe-in for success in the move.

11. *Risk-taking.* If you like taking a few high-stakes chances

instead of always going for lower-payoff sure things, the transfer may be just what you're looking for.

12. *Social initiative.* If you wait around for introductions, you may find the new place lonely, and the new job not to your liking.

13. *Quality of family interaction.* If you see your kids only when you bail them out of jail, and your spouse drives you to drink, you may lack the emotional support at home to do well on the job.

14. *Pre-eminence of job.* Whose job is more important, yours or your spouse's? If both you and your spouse agree that it's yours, and the transfer is for your job, your chances are better than if you're the one who takes a dive on his or her career.

15. *Transferability of spouse's work.* If your spouse can get a job at the same level as her or his old job, your chances are better than the opposite situation—wherein the unlucky spouse drops down to selling hamburgers at McDonalds or hangs around the house, waiting to yell resentfully at the employed one when he or she returns after a hard day at the office.

According to Dr. Michael Tucker, a senior VP at Moran, Stahl & Boyer, for those people who score well on these dimensions, "the up-to-speed time can be cut by 15 to 20 percent." Since the average time to get back to the old rate after a move is over eight months, cutting out a month or two of extra problems could be the difference between keeping a job and wishing you had stayed at home.

KEY POINTS

- The scramble to fit in is one of the more sinister ordeals because it strikes at your self-confidence. Keep your confidence bolstered by remembering your past achievements (make a list if it helps!).

- Some questions top management will be asking themselves

The Scramble To Fit In

about where you fit in are ones over which you have very little control.

- The other questions they'll be asking will have to do with your track record, your economic indispensability, and involvement on key committees—areas where you have a *great* deal of control.
- Flexibility is the best attitude to have if you want to stay—and move up—at your company.
- You may be able to fit in by relocating, but this may require more flexibility than you or your family can muster.

THE SIXTH ORDEAL
The Tough Sell

Nearly everyone who comes out okay in takeovers has taken the initiative to sell their skills not only to the new boss, but to key customers as well. And nearly all who kick themselves later do so because they hadn't been active enough in doing this—either they had been lulled into a false sense of security by the new or old owners, or they hadn't taken the initiative to see what other opportunities were available or what other information was available about their new bosses.

But how do you sell yourself to the new bosses, especially when you may not *like* them? This presents one of the most unpleasant ordeals of all for the manager trying not only to get through the day but to move ahead.

Staying Close to the Customers

For people with access to customers, according to Ward Naughton, a consultant with Edgar, Dunn and Conover in San Francisco, "the most effective thing is to cover their markets and be very visible with the client. The new players—bosses—are looking to the customers to tell them who's good, so the way to sell yourself to the new owners is to put aside your own personal uncertainty and continue to sell the combined company."

Naughton bases his advice on his own experience and observations when he was a calling officer (in lending) at a major bank, which we'll call Major Bank, that was taken over by another, which we'll call Big Bank.

When the merger is first announced, the company is most visible, with press coverage and torrents of rumors. That's when the customer has the most questions about his own situation. This provides people who are in touch with the customers with a greater opportunity than ever to make their case. "There were reports of certain banks going after the customer," reports Naughton, "and the acquiring bank had to be very visible because the customers were asking similar questions to those being asked inside the acquired bank." Some of the questions on the customers' minds: Do I fit into the new strategy? Do they offer the products I need? How important are differences in the skills of the people? How well do I know senior management?

"You have a choice," Naughton continues, "either you muddle around and say I'm not going to try to get any more business until things settle down, or you go out and try to bring in more business. The people who were most attractive to [Big Bank] were those who did this, as well as those with established reputations in the industry."

Did this strategy work for him? Apparently so. "I was one of a small number of people who were offered a job in the lending side," he reports. And it was precisely by staying close to the customer that this came about. "I had a client, a Fortune 500 company, in which the top financial officer, the treasurer, wrote [Big Bank] a letter advising them to offer me a job, saying I had handled the account well—and this was done without any request of mine."

So your job can sometimes be preserved if the new owners want to keep a customer happy. The new owners can get sold on you by the very people you have been selling.

Of course, the new owners still may not retain you if they believe you aren't very good. So the trick is to make them believe you *are* good. Your reputation for quality can, to some degree, be established beyond your own company. In many industries, people are or can be highly visible. "If there's a bank financing of a large acquisition, all the banks are there," says Naughton, adding, "You're sitting next to the guy from what will become the new owners, only you don't even know your bank is up for sale. So my advice is to do your

The Tough Sell

job with the intensity that your company could be yanked out from under you tomorrow."

Another calling officer at this same acquired Major Bank also was retained by Big Bank as a result of management's asking around. "I had been at the bank for 14 years prior to the acquisition," he said, "involved as a major lender to large corporations. Then in '83 I was sent to London for two and a half years, so when the sale was announced, I didn't know many people from the new owners. But the corporate people at the new owners asked around town, asked the corporations I had been dealing with."

Apparently, he got some good references, judging by what happened next. "My first official contact was in an interview by a man who was only one or two levels above me," said this calling officer. He added, "He interviewed everyone else in his office, but he said he wanted to have drinks with me. Over drinks he said I had been identified as one they wanted to keep, but said the rules of the game were that they couldn't officially offer jobs at that time in case the deal didn't come about. But he asked me not to run around town looking for another job."

To whom did they go for references? He explained: "Principally an informal network, mainly in the community and to some extent in the bank. At one point they asked me what I thought of others. So it's important to align oneself with the right people."

Although this calling officer arrived at his new bank presold, he did not take this to mean that he was secure. He took exactly the opposite position. "Once you start in your new job in the organization," he said, "you should quickly establish credibility because you're under much more severe scrutiny than before, so you don't have to trip very hard to trip all the way."

His advice was the same as that from the others who were successful in these ordeals: "Work very hard." Your previous owner may have had a very high regard for you—this banker referred to it as "tremendous personal capital." But this kind of capital doesn't work like cash; it isn't fully transferable. "You have to build up personal capital again," said the banker, "protect existing business, demonstrate good management skills, bring in good loans."

As we have seen repeatedly in this book, takeover targets are often companies that have done badly, have essentially turned themselves around by making major investments and cutting costs, but have not yet received the payoffs for these investments in the form of profits. So for everyone not fully in the know, they still appear to be doing badly. Almost inevitably this means their stock price has not yet caught up with their potential financial success.

Although this unfortunate lag in the market can be devastating for companies, it can offer great career opportunities to managers. For those with access to the customer, the turnaround period provides even more opportunity to sell themselves to senior management and achieve visibility in the industry.

For example, Ward Naughton reports that at the time of the takeover:

> Most of the people still there were the ones who had toughed it out during the period when our bank had experienced significant losses. The old owner took the hit on our losses, and some calling people were fired or quit. The headhunters came in to try to get the good people because they knew the bank would go through cost containment. But some people, many young like me, stayed. I could have gone across the street to another bank, but I saw this as a major opportunity to help turn the bank around. I did it for the experience—there isn't necessarily more money in it. Here you are a VP and suddenly you're dealing with senior management more than you would otherwise. Bad times can be an excellent opportunity.
>
> Some of the things I learned there I now have an opportunity to apply in a consulting role. For example, in a problem institution, the focus becomes internal, the paper load increases—more reports are required. I'm able from firsthand experience to tell top management that the hidden but catastrophic cost of their sudden increase in the load of paperwork is to keep people away from the customers, which makes the problems worse. I advise top management to use outside help, and not to bog down the sales people.
>
> I think [people] working for an organization today should have in their minds the possibility of a merger, and should be aware of what story they should tell, what is their book of success.

Selling Yourself: Tips from Outplacement While You're Still In

This banker has a good idea. But it needs elaboration. Virtually everyone retained in a takeover goes through a retention interview at one point or another. The usual procedure is that the employees, having worked hard at the acquired company, suddenly, through no fault of their own, have to struggle to get an interview with someone they don't know from a company they don't understand, but which suddenly has taken control of their lives. They then try to explain themselves to a person who may not know what they're talking about, and may not even care. Potential retainees go in, ill at ease, sometimes panicked, and often hostile. They try to suppress these feelings, usually fail to do so, and usually fail to keep their jobs. Many, maybe even most, people are not good at these things. The evidence is that so many ultimately do not get retained.

What you have to do is make a good impression at the retention interview. Since takeovers have become so common, you should consider this a serious project long before you even know there is the possibility of a retention interview. One way to triumph at these interviews is to follow some of the same procedures used by outplacement firms—mock interviews. Only instead of mock *job* interviews, you need to do mock retention interviews.

Outplacement companies and their volunteer, nonprofit counterparts, Forty Plus chapters, give a lot of advice on handling job interviews. For example, Pat Slater, executive director of Forty Plus in Houston, suggests writing up a list of 25 accomplishments. In doing so, according to Mrs. Slater, you should "take credit for your own unique contributions to the bottom line." This involves figuring out, and concisely stating, what your contributions have been. Do this for 25 distinct functional items and you'll definitely get the knack of it. Also, virtually every adviser urges that you keep the list up to date.

Tedious? Sure. A valuable idea? Both successful managers and those who counsel the bumped say it is. As Ward Naughton says, it forms a personal "book of success" that you can pitch at the retention interview. "It will give you confidence when you pitch yourself," says Pat Slater. The point is to do it *now*, so you don't have to do it in outplacement or at Forty Plus.

Once you've got your book of success, how do you actually pitch it? "The more experience people have had at pitching anything, the better they'll be at pitching themselves," says Pat Slater. She puts her view into practice by sending everyone who joins her chapter of Forty Plus out into the business community to pitch Forty Plus. The idea is to get business backing for the organization, but the real value for the pitchers is to get exposure in the business world, so they're pitching themselves at the same time they're touting the organization. Many of the unemployed managers who join are scientists, not always the gladhanding, extroverted type. Obviously, many of these people find the experience of pitching a product—even a worthwhile one such as a group like Forty Plus—to be very painful. "It's interesting to watch them turn around," says Slater. "They get an insight into seeing other jobs; geologists become salespeople."

If you're lucky enough not to need Forty Plus, where do you get comparable selling experience? "Join Toastmasters," says Slater, "so you can learn how to speak and make presentations. Shop around for the most congenial group; some are more structured, others more laid back."

Joining an outfit like Toastmasters leads to Slater's third suggestion. "When networking, you must go outside of your field because you never know where you'll find people who will be most helpful to you." She urges the same salesperson's no-stone-unturned approach to looking for a mentor within your company right now, because "there's always someone there who is concerned for you."

Sid North, 44, the executive VP of the Orange County, California, Forty Plus, also has some tips for managers facing a retention interview. He cautions them to first appreciate the problem for the person doing the interviewing. Says North:

> Most upper and middle level executives are not good interviewers. They're not comfortable; they don't like doing it because it's flesh buying. People hire or retain you because you can do the job and they like you. Concern about qualifications goes out the window after two minutes since they've decided by then either that you can do it or you can't. So the issue for them is whether they like you. Since the boss in a turnaround will have to spend more time with you than with his own wife, he wants to know if he can stand putting in that time. It's fair.

Sometimes the retention interview isn't with the person for whom you'll be working, but with someone from personnel. Personnel interviewers have one thing in mind—don't ever recommend the wrong person. They bury their mistakes that would have worked out in the outplacement office, so no one will ever call them on the carpet for these errors. By contrast, recommending someone who turns out to be a drug addict, a child molester, or an embezzler could send the interviewer himself to the outplacement office. Of course, most people are none of these three things; however, simply referring someone who gets retained but doesn't work out could

The Tough Sell

also lead to trouble for a personnel interviewer. This fact nearly assures that personnel interviewers will adopt the "better safe than sorry" approach to retention interviewing, which means that they feel they have a real incentive to nail as many people as they can. Since this means they must fire or reject a lot of people, they want to get as quickly as they can to the word, "Next!" To avoid wasting time, they've come up with the "stress" interview.

Sid North's Forty Plus chapter has been collecting a list of particularly nasty stress questions, which it then fires at its own members at mock interviews:

Question: What can you do for us that someone else can't?

Your answer: Whatever you do, don't start chopping down the competition. Build up your own qualifications instead.

Question: Why have you changed jobs so frequently?

Your answer: There is no pat answer. "Never lie," says North, "but you don't have to be so bloody honest." You might say you've been in consulting, and so have still worked for some of these companies in effect.

Question: What are your three biggest failures?

Your answer: When answering this question, remember the rule of the Three-Card Monte card sharps on the streets of New York: Never pay off. Don't admit to having any failures; they'll be taken down and used against you.

Question: Why did you leave your last job?

Your answer: With this one, you should remember the dictum of the corrupt political machine, Tammany Hall in New York: Claim everything, concede nothing, and if you lose, allege fraud. If this is a retention interview the answer is obvious: You left to come to a better job, here. If you're unemployed, advises North, "Don't bare your soul."

Question: What kind of salary are you worth?

Your answer: Since the answer depends on the position, don't give a figure. Ask the interviewer to describe the position.

For really sadistic personnel interviewers, the ones who keep psychologically fit by pulling the wings off butterflies, there is always the ultimate stress question:

Question: If you were a flower, what kind would you be?

Your answer: Give the single correct response, "A weed, it grows anywhere." Don't slug the interviewer.

While you're in this interview, advises North, be very courteous, treat the interviewer in a professional manner, and remember to smile. To help you achieve this finesse, you might shop around for a place that has video cameras you can practice in front of. Try a Forty Plus chapter, but don't lie; tell them you still have a job, but are worried.

Selling Yourself to the Right Person

"Go as high up as you can get, because the situation is in a state of flux. Try to get as close to the CEO as you can," advises Jewell Westerman, 53, a vice president of Temple, Barker, & Sloane, Inc., a Massachusetts-based management consulting firm.

"I don't agree," says a senior executive in the communications industry who has survived a takeover. "How do you get an audience with the CEO, who is, in all likelihood, tied up in meetings and even more inaccessible than ever? And if you jump the chain of command you could put the mark of death on yourself," she adds.

But let's say you do get to the CEO. What do you do when you get there? Tell him how great his new set-up is, according to some consultants. For example, Westerman advises, "Demonstrate your enthusiasm and willingness to work hard for it. If you don't believe in it, you won't survive anyway, at least if you can't come around to supporting the new direction."

But the senior executive in communications disagrees. "It's not going to make for pleasant day-to-day dealings and may even appear traitorous to so heartily endorse the takeover," she says from personal experience.

Although the communications executive has succeeded without following the sort of advice Westerman and others give, quite a few managers have succeeded precisely because they *did* do something along the lines of what Westerman advises. Somehow they were able to see the good things about the raiders. If you think what the raiders do is not to your liking, you're probably not going to succeed in a company from which they are squeezing out the equity.

According to this line of thinking, you must whip up enthusiasm about seeing managers fired only a few years from retirement. If this doesn't work, you have to somehow get enthusiastic about "the stockholders." Unfortunately the typical stockholder is no longer the grey-haired old lady in Duluth trudging through the snow to the mailbox to pick up her dividend check. The typical stockholder today is, instead, a somewhat colorless, faceless bu-

The Tough Sell

reaucrat who administers institutional investment portfolios. If you can't get rah-rah over them, try "the entrepreneurs" in the set-up. If the fact that they are really speculators and asset strippers who go by the high-falutin name "arbitrageurs" throws a wet blanket on the party, there's always that *new* chestnut, "future competitiveness." That's the one to sink your teeth into. Think of it as the bullet you're biting when you make your pitch.

"Most people don't get a lot of satisfaction out of their jobs today," says Westerman, who adds that although many of the big corporate mergers are undeniably flops, "there are a lot of subsidiaries that are sold that work." This, of course, is true, and it provides you with a way to steel yourself for what you must do next. Look for the economic strengths and see whether you can believe in them. For example, sales may be larger, it will be a bigger company with a stronger position in the marketplace, it may be more efficient and a stronger competitor. "There must appear to be competitive advantages," says Westerman, "or the merger wouldn't have gone through in the first place." The apparent competitive advantages will inevitably be expressed in some of the press releases. Whether the competitive advantages are the true reason for the merger or it was simply for asset stripping, tax boondoggles or the ego needs of the CEO, need not be addressed at this conversation with the highest-up boss you can corner.

According to many consultants, you must take this favorable position regarding the merger when talking with high-ups in the company, despite the fact that we know from the McKinsey study that, in general, it is just plain false. You must pretend or believe that this merger will be the exception. However, keep in mind that not everyone believes that extolling the merger is a good strategy. "Your boss may be even more adamantly opposed to the takeover than you are," says the communications executive who succeeded in one of these things. As in other ordeals we have discussed, there are different schools of thought regarding what is best.

Once you've touted the economic advantages of the merger to your boss, if you can't get hold of anybody higher up, what else do you say? "Tell him 'Here's how I can contribute to this process,' " advises Westerman.

Now comes the hard part; he may not have the slightest idea what you're talking about. Your job now is to get your pitch to the right person. Fay, 30, did this. She worked at the same acquired bank we discussed earlier. She was assigned to be interviewed by a gentleman from the acquirer, but she realized after a few minutes that he was the wrong guy. She explains:

I was in a peculiar situation. The merger was announced in February, but the month before I had been transferred out of the division calling on major corporations to a new division, which dealt with financial institutions—insurance companies, brokerage houses, and other banks. A couple of years earlier, the acquiring bank had closed down a similar department, so we were obviously lame ducks. Customers would say to me, "Why should I start a new relationship with you?" We just tried to hang on to the business that we had. But the interviewer perceived me to be a financial institutions person even though for four years [previous to that] one month I had worked calling on Fortune 1000 companies.

So what did she do? "I had to really emphasize what exactly it was I did," she explains. "I spent a lot of time explaining my particular portfolio. The key was getting out of the first interview into a second one with the right person, and the interviewer was kind enough to route me to the right person."

However, this didn't completely solve her problem. Fay's portfolio was in paradise—Hawaii, the Big Island and Maui. "A dirty job, but somebody had to do it," she joked. The man from the acquiring company, which had no business in Hawaii, assumed it was strictly a vacation place and wanted to know how she could justify spending the bank's money going there four times a year for extended visits. "And because of federal regulations I couldn't tell him how profitable it was—the merger hadn't been officially concluded," she recalls.

She couldn't tell the acquiring company, but the customers could, and did. "They called three or more customers for each person," she says, adding, "Each of them called me after talking to them, which was nice." They knew her well. "Hawaii isn't the most dynamic market place, you spend a lot of time handholding the customers," she remarks.

But it worked. "I talked to them the first week in May," she recalls, adding, "The next week they talked to the customers, and the week after, the second gentleman I talked to asked me for a beer and told me I had a job. The people who didn't get hired (retained) found out the day the merger was official. But most of them figured it out beforehand because the people around them were getting offers."

So she's back on the Hawaii beat. "But if I come back with a tan, I'll lose my job. It's not so much fun wearing pantyhose in Hawaii," she concludes.

Fay was forbidden by law to play her highest card at these retention interviews—bringing something to the party. Fortunately for her, the Hawaiian customers who had regaled her with stories of their kids getting into college acted in the finest tradition of Hawaiian hospitality and brought something to the party *for* her—a statement to the new management of how much money their business was worth and how much they liked Fay. In effect, Fay was bringing that business to the party, which was her selling point, even if the law required it to be a soft-sell.

General Tips from an Expert

"Do something dramatic" advises headhunter Robert Half, author of several books on getting a job. How dramatic? "Not a major thing, minor," adds Half, who elaborates about his own experience many years ago. "When I got a job after I left public accounting, I found a device which would hold four-by-eight-inch papers," says Half. "By moving a sliding gizmo, you could get comparative financial data by exposing a column on the left and then one on the right. It doesn't sound like much now, with computerized spreadsheets, but it made a big impression at the time."

The idea isn't that you demonstrate in seconds that you're worth billions of dollars to the new owners, but that you can be innovative and helpful. "There must be hundreds of small things that you could use for this purpose," says Half.

Half has other pointers for those selling themselves: Look a little better dressed, slightly but not dramatically better than your old colleagues in the acquired company. "At a meeting after an acquisition," says Half, "those doing the acquiring looked more corporate than the acquired. But the smart ones among the acquired quickly got their looks in order. It's better to change to look like the people in the dominant group than like those in your old group." What if the latter view you as a traitor? "So what," says Half, "you'll be there to wave good-bye to them."

"Remember that you are always being interviewed, even if it's an unconscious act on the part of the interviewer," says Half, "so always drop hints in a modest way of how good you are." But how do you avoid making yourself unbelievable by always tooting your own horn? According to Half, you should slip in the key data in the middle of an anecdote that is ostensibly about something else. A good lead-in line is something like, "I have to tell you a funny thing that happened. . . ." Then in the course of telling the "funny thing" you also slip in the good part about what you're doing.

"Punctuality and attendance records are important, particularly when new people are in charge," says Half. "No excuses," he concludes. "Don't bring personal problems to the office."

Have a pleasant smile, not a laughing look as if you're telling a joke," warns Half, who even has advice on how to pull this one off: "Think of the word 'smile' and you do it a little bit. Practice it in the mirror and you'll see," he suggests.

"Keep a personal personnel file," advises Half. "Every time you have an achievement, put a note on it in your own personnel file," he adds. What for? This helps you to recite what you've done when you are called in for the retention interview.

KEY POINTS

- To move ahead after the takeover, it's important to put aside feelings of dislike for or anxiety about the new owners and sell yourself and your achievements to them instead.
- Equally important, you need to stay close to the customers or clients, as the case may be, and get them to sell *you* to the new management.
- Always make sure, however, that you're selling yourself to the right person.
- Prepare yourself for a retention interview, even before you have the remotest idea that there will be one.
- Join public speaking organizations to practice your ability to make pitches.
- Adapt to the look of the new management.
- Don't go around with the mask of doom on your face. Project a look of confidence and ease, which means smiling, even when it hurts.

7
THE SEVENTH ORDEAL
The Backstabbers

During the rumors, chaos, side-taking, and desperate maneuvering to fit in, still another ordeal faces the embattled manager: People he thought were his friends turn out not to be. This is hardly surprising. The takeover has provoked a nasty game of too many managers and not enough desks. As one senior manager who had survived three takeovers put it, "You have to assume no one's your friend or colleague in this situation. You're trying to save your financial highknee, your family, your career."

One of the most insidious parts of this ordeal is that you may not even know the backstabbing has happened to you until long after the fact, by which time you can't do anything to protect yourself.

The backstabbing might have occurred at a meeting you didn't even know took place because, officially, it never happened. For example, in the chapter on finding out who the new bosses are, we stressed the importance of finding a sympathetic person in the acquiring company and going to him with the aim of making your case. This meeting might not be in his office, but over drinks after work. Suppose a potential rival arranged this meeting. Your name came up. Would you find out right away that he had said anything disparaging, or damned you with faint praise, or simply said that he didn't know anything about you because he had never heard anything one way or the other?

No Crime or Simply No Fingerprints?

Perhaps nothing unfavorable in any way was said about you. However, let's say you get dumped. The natural assumption is that someone fingered you, and people spend a lot of time trying to guess who it was. Often they're wrong. Toronto outplacement consultant Robin T. Hazell has an interesting observation that is relevant to this point. "We do reference checking for people and give the client, who is in outplacement, the flavor without saying who said what. Ofttimes the client believes that Jones said something bad or Smith something good, whereas it could have been the reverse," reports Hazell. "I don't think backstabbing is as common as people think it is," he concludes.

An example of a man who says he was unjustly blamed for backstabbing is Joe, 42, a VP of marketing at a large Ohio petrochemicals company that was being looked over for purchase by a Japanese buyer. Through negotiations with top management of the petrochemicals company, the potential Japanese buyers put together an organization chart. Joe was on it, although moved over to a staff position. He explained what happened:

> I wasn't privy to the names going into the boxes—I knew who they were, but I didn't make the decision. A fellow who worked for me (he reported to me but we really all worked together—it was pretty informal) was not on the final chart and thought I should have pushed for a slot for him. It ruined our friendship for a year. But I knew his relationship with the guy doing the picking and choosing, and it wasn't good. He didn't have as high an opinion of this guy as a manager as he did of some others. So I didn't push it.

Was this backstabbing? It's in the eye of the beholder. Apparently the man who felt stabbed eventually decided he hadn't been, or else he forgave his assailant, since, two companies later, he hired Joe as a consultant. Incidentally, the whole thing came to nothing in the petrochemicals case since the Japanese purchase fell through.

Who Did You Say Was Carrying a Poison Umbrella?

Some backstabbings are unquestionably real, and the rest of this chapter will detail a number of common ones, together with the medicine used by the people who were stabbed, and in some instances the medicine they *wish* they had used. In some cases, they are talking from their hospital beds, far away from the scene of the crime. In other cases, they have been able to fight their assailants to a draw, and in still others, they have turned the knives on the assailants who got cut by their own blades.

In the highly charged atmosphere of the takeover, where paranoia can become a contagious disease, some people become the Typhoid Marys of office paranoia. A few years ago in London, an intelligence officer attached as a diplomat to an Eastern European embassy murdered another diplomat by walking by him on the street and puncturing him with an umbrella that had a poisoned tip. The story got sensational press coverage, and for a while in normally level-headed London, quite a few people were eying all folded, swinging umbrellas carried by well-dressed gentlemen with some suspicion. Much of London had been made paranoid. This has corporate significance.

"One of the best ways to zap [an opponent] is to try to make [him] paranoid," says Richard B. Warren, president of Cole, Warren and Long, Inc., Philadelphia consultants. Obviously, he's not recommending this sort of thing, but he's seen it happen and he advises top management on the best ways to keep it from happening. Warren explains the usual technique: "Someone comes into your office. 'Don't tell anybody,' he says, 'but I've just heard that you're on the skids; you're in deep trouble.' The guy does this in a helping way, but he tries to make you paranoid. If he makes you totally paranoid, he knows you'll mess up. His goal is to raise your anxiety. This happens at all levels of the organization."

This happened in a Florida food processing company that had been taken over by a large Louisiana-based, family-owned conglomerate. A manager in his mid-fifties was one of the first ordered axed by the new owners, who simply didn't like him. But this raised problems for the president of the company taken over, because the man who was about to be fired was extremely good at his job; in fact, he was viewed as one of the best people in the company. So the president was worried about a possible age discrimination suit. He therefore went out of his way to make sure the firing was done correctly. George, the VP who worked out the severance agreement, came into the office of Abe, the VP of personnel, who got stiffed with doing the firing and totally fabricated a story. He whispered to Abe, "The president is really hot under the collar. You really lost points. He thinks you said things that could leave us open to a big, precedent-setting lawsuit. I covered for you, but don't mention this to anyone, especially the president." Why did George want to do in Abe? He knew there were other firings coming, and he wanted to be in charge of them, so he wanted to discredit Abe and get him out of the way.

Naturally, Abe did go to the president, which only helped George the Knife, who had already dropped hints in the president's ear of Abe's paranoia. The president called in George, who, when called on the carpet, easily defended himself by saying, "You know, I always told you Abe misunderstands things. His paranoia has blown this whole thing way out of proportion." This was the perfect response, since the president had no way of knowing the truth, but would simply be watching both of these persons. George, of course, would make sure he was perfectly cool. But Abe was very likely to be ultra sensitive, and perhaps show signs of paranoia, confirming George's claim to the president. "Human behavior is such that one tends to believe the first person who tells him something," says Dick Warren.

In this sort of backstabbing, any attempt to defend yourself in an honorable way is almost certain to make things worse for you, since it appears to confirm the thrust of the backstabber's story, which is that you are paranoid. You'd be much better off doing one of two things: (1) nothing, ignore the whole thing; or (2) figure out some way to try the same stratagem on the guy who backstabbed you.

Incidentally, another version of the poison umbrella ploy can happen in any situation where those given the paranoia-inducing information can't go back to double check it, for whatever reason. This is quite common in takeovers, where double checking would require contacting a far-away office at corporate headquarters. This happened when a Southern California manufacturing company was taken over by an Omaha-based conglomerate. The conglomerate immediately had every Southern California functional underling report directly to a VP in Omaha. As a result, the comparable California VPs started losing authority. They were actually being controlled by their own subordinates, who would say in total honesty, "I just got the word from corporate headquarters." In fact the California subordinates didn't always talk to the Omaha VPs, but to the Omaha subordinates of the VPs. These "gentlemen" did not always give accurate information regarding their boss' intentions.

All the California VPs had to do was pick up the phone and verify what was what, but many did not, out of a growing paranoid fear that they would be viewed as *paranoid*. As a result, many of the California VPs, acting on the wrong information, made mistakes and were fired. The Omaha subordinates then got promoted into those jobs. As one manager who did very well in making a California VP paranoid and then getting his job explained, "Anyone with balls could take over."

Incidentally, this version of the poisoned umbrella ploy illustrates an interesting point about some of the firings resulting from takeovers. Quite a few top managers at the acquiring company can play the role of Pontius Pilate, saying of any given manager in an acquired company far away, "I see nothing wrong with this man." He might be perfectly happy to see something wrong, if someone with initiative cares to show it to him, and a lower ranking person at corporate headquarters might be happy to do so.

Tied to a Rolling Log as It Heads for the Sawmill Blade

Recall the famous silent movie serial, "The Perils of Pauline." In countless episodes, the black-hatted villain ties poor Pauline to a log as it heads for the spinning blade. In the post-takeover situation, you may not be surprised at all the logs laying around just waiting to be sawed. But these are the easy logs to keep your eye on. Some others might be a bit rotten and waterlogged, so they're floating with just a hint of a piece of old bark showing. Resourceful executives can spot them, roll them over, and trade them in deals. "Buying favoritism through log rolling is a favorite ploy," says Dick Warren. "An executive in the acquiring company will say to one in the acquired, 'There'll be a lot of changes in St. Louis. If you help me get done what I want done, you'll do well.' Implied is that he'll die if he doesn't help."

A fact that is often forgotten in the wave of takeovers in the corporate world is that log rolling happens in the public sector too. In fact, it has been taking place quite a lot lately in local government agencies. Due to cutbacks in federal funding, local agencies have been consolidated and entire programs shifted from one agency to another, sometimes several times. Equivalent to this would be a corporation's selling off a strategic business unit.

Ellen, 46, got caught up in one of these agency consolidations and log rollings. She worked in a large city in the Pacific Northwest for a municipal agency that had several federally funded programs. Ellen was the director of one program. Located at a local hospital, it gave preschool training to handicapped children and was the largest program of its kind in the state. The program was more than a Project Headstart for the handicapped, since it offered not only education, but also physical therapy, social services for the poor families that needed the program, and psychological counseling for both the kids and their families.

But due to a series of federal budget cutbacks, the program was constantly being starved for funds, with resulting service cutbacks and complaints to City Hall. As a result, Ellen was the fifth director in the past four years. In a further attempt to save money, John, the county official in charge of the program, decided to consolidate the assessment programs. From now on, instead of each hospital running its own assessment of its kids, all the children initially would be evaluated at a central location, which turned out to be at Ellen's hospital and under Ellen's direction. This put her in a conflict of interest, since she potentially could refer an excessive number of children to her own program to guarantee that her budget didn't get cut any further.

John, the county official, proposed a solution. The assessment program would remain in place, but under the auspices of another city agency. "He tipped me to one," reported Ellen, who spent the next six months working out the details of the transfer.

Then came the first hints that there were other logs floating in those waters. Ellen reported that John told her

> ... he was getting inquiries from other agencies that wanted the program. Two months later, he announced that a different agency would take over. I phoned the head of the other agency and asked for a copy of their proposal. 'Proposal?,' she replied, 'What proposal?' The other agency was helping in providing care for the homeless, which caused a community uproar over the deplorable places in which they were housing these people. The reputation of that agency is terrible—they're cheap and they give terrible services. My program was a payoff to keep them happy by giving them some good publicity, although I could never prove this.

Ellen was, of course, strapped to the log of the assessment center, but the local bureaucratic sawmill soon took care of that.

"Everyone, including me," was initially retained, said Ellen. She added:

> I was still the director, but my job changed a lot—I lost control of the budget. They led me to believe I was going to be kept on, but then they started reducing the therapy. When I complained to the head of the agency, I was called on the carpet, but told not to look for another job. Two days short of the probationary period, I was fired. In fact, of the original staff of 30, only 3 are left. I was the only one fired. The county administrator [John] wanted to hold onto the integrity of the Center, but somewhere along the line the pressure on the homeless issue forced him into the compromise. Because I was a thorn in his side, he had me fired.

What could Ellen have done to head off this problem? At her level in the bureaucracy, she probably could not have tried some log rolling of her own, offering the county official a better deal. But one strategy she *could* have used is open only to those in the public sector. She could use local politics to throw an even bigger log in the way of the one she was on. This would block her path to the sawmill, and buy time, which is essentially all one can do in a takeover environment. Ellen agrees that this would have been a good idea. "In hindsight, I probably should have organized the parents and, through them, mobilized local politicians," she said. Had she succeeded in bringing in her own political pressure, she might have found the bigger log. The risk is that she would have branded herself as a political troublemaker. This would have been true win or lose, but if she lost she would have been viewed as a weak political troublemaker.

The Switchblade

One reason Ellen had been reluctant to organize the parents was that she could be charged with making a pure power grab. "A naked power grab is very rare," says consultant Warren. "You always have to look like the good guy." This is why few people are foolish or desperate enough to allow the shining blade to glint in the sunlight. This fact can be used to spot knife-wielders. If you see someone being an excessive good guy, you often have the giveaway that he is packing a big, nasty switchblade. "Watch out for people who use subterfuge to become indispensable," warns Dick Warren.

This happened in a Birmingham, Alabama, insurance company after it was taken over by a Miami conglomerate. A VP left immediately for a better job and was replaced with a new man from corporate in Miami. Two directors reported to him. Both were gentlemanly, but one was a first-rate manager and quite kind, while the other was not such a great manager and quite ruthless to boot. However, the latter did not tip his utter ruthlessness to the new VP. Instead he said to him, "You're brand new and have a lot on your mind. I can help with things until you get your footing." He became indispensable for the reduction in force, and the kinder director soon found himself directed to outplacement.

The knife the ruthless director wielded in this case was to *go by the book*. He was in underwriting, and he was afraid that his unit would be folded into a comparable unit at another insurance company the conglomerate owned. The other director was in marketing, and had put together a very effective department. So the ruthless director simply got the okay of the new VP for new, more cautious, approval criteria. He sold it to him on the idea that in the post-takeover environment, they couldn't afford to run any extra risk—a standard argument. However, this devastated the marketing department, which looked bad even though it made underwriting look good. So the entire marketing department was dumped and folded in with the one from the other insurance company. Underwriting was left alone.

The "going by the book" ploy can be used by technical departments to cut down other departments, so that the choice of which to keep will be obvious. Research and development can cut up production by writing up new policies and procedures that are clearly economically advantageous on paper, but have the effect of screwing up production. This is not a time when production wants to look like it has problems. Computer systems can slice up nearly anyone simply by introducing a complex but more efficient system that the users can't handle at first. This forces the computer department to get more people, which means other departments will have to be cut back even further.

The lesson here is that many backstabbings happen to entire departments; they get executed as a group. So you must be alert to who has the ear of the new bosses, and leave the company before the blade cuts down your department.

Getting Your Right Arm Cut Off

Indispensable managers are those the new owners must keep, either for good economic reasons or because they literally have blackmail power over the company—they know where the bodies are buried. Frank was in the position of being indispensable for the latter reason. He was the drilling division controller at an oil company headquartered in a small town outside of New Orleans and recently taken over by an investment group. So many corners had been cut to get regulatory approval and skirt government regulations that Frank was too dangerous to let loose. He knew too much. Since he had actively participated in cutting those corners, he was in no hurry to tell the authorities. But sudden hard times and the shock of being fired could change all that. The company simply couldn't fire him or cut his pay.

Just as Frank knew too much, so did a long-time rival, his boss, Charlie, the chief financial officer. He had never liked Frank, but was never able to fire him for the same reason that the new owners couldn't fire him (and couldn't fire Charlie, for that matter). But now Charlie was allowed a little more latitude; the new owners permitted him to cut Frank up a bit.

Charlie waited for Frank to go on one of his frequent trips to the drilling fields. In this case, the trip lasted nearly four weeks instead of the usual two. As was usual during these long absences, the drilling division controller's office was run by Mollie, 54, his immediate subordinate. "I was his right arm. Without me he couldn't run the department while he was away for such a long time," said Mollie. Charlie knew that this was true. Two days after Frank left on his trip, "they gave me the boot, just like that," reported Mollie as she snapped her fingers. She added, "They wouldn't even let me clean out my desk without Charlie and a security guard standing over me. I think they were afraid I'd walk off with incriminating documents." Frank didn't find out about it for three weeks. He was furious, but Mollie was off the premises by then and there was nothing he could do. He had been effectively stabbed in the back and rendered ineffective in his job.

Two months later, Charlie switched him out of his department to one headed by a member of the investment group, who had a new title, the chief accounting officer. Frank would work on special projects, which turned out to be not much. "All he does is try to alienate me, hoping I'll leave," said Frank, adding, "I can't relocate because the housing market is too depressed, and there are no jobs in the oil business around here now. I've got a baby coming so I've got to keep on working until they lay me off." He's safe there, since this won't be until the statute of limitations expires. In the meantime, he has to face daily humiliation. As you can see, being indispensable because you know the dope can be hazardous to your career. However, being economically indispensable generally helps move your career forward, as noted in the previous chapter.

Wasn't Mollie indispensable too, for the same reason Frank was? "Sure," she said, "but I'd have to get Frank to corroborate my statements, which I can't assume he'll do. I've thought of suing because I'm 54, a woman, and black. But I can't prove discrimination because they haven't filled my job with a man or anyone younger or whiter. They're not that stupid."

So unscrupulous people can stab even the indispensable in the back. The weak ones they can stab and kick out. The stronger ones they leave as walking wounded.

How could Frank have countered the actions of Charlie and the others? He'd have to play hardball, actually verbally threatening what has so far only been implicit and unstated. Even if this worked, it would brand him as a troublemaker and guarantee that he'd never get another corporate job. Who wants to hire a blackmailer? So his indispensability keeps his paycheck coming in, but doesn't exactly make him sing out with joy. The lesson here is not to count on indispensability, but at the first hint of possible trouble, get out to another job if you can.

No More Knives Backing You Up

"The most common form of backstabbing," says consultant and psychotherapist Doug Lind, "is when your mentor stops paying attention. You are out there without the champion, and you become aware [of] how alone you are."

What can you do to set things right? According to Lind, "If there's a solution, it is almost always to find another champion. An awful lot of people resist doing this, believing that it's cheating. They think politics is bad, forgetting the root of the word, which translates as *community*."

Finding a new mentor, however, isn't so easy in the post-takeover set-up. Brad, 41, the assistant treasurer of a California offshore oil drilling company, discovered this unhappy fact the hard way, but was nonetheless able to take great advantage of the new mentor relationship.

When Brad's company was taken over by an insurance company, his mentor and boss, the treasurer—who was also CFO—jumped to a better job at a major transportation company. This left Brad in the lurch, since his mentor either couldn't or wouldn't offer to take him along. The takeover happened and his boss left just as the price of oil peaked and started a long slide down to $10 a barrel.

So there was a job opening for the person who would be Brad's new boss. Brad himself wasn't in the running, but two of his friends were. "There was also one dark horse, brought in by the new owners, who always snidely discredited the other two at meetings. If one of them came up with an idea, he'd ridicule it," recalls Brad. The dark horse had had a big job at one of the lender banks, and as Brad's company began to have more and more trouble with debt, the dark horse became increasingly powerful. Eventually he got the CFO job.

"I tried to find a new champion, and I did, the CEO and chairman, but he couldn't do anything because the people the banks wanted were now calling the tune. There was no way you could prove it, but they had their knighted people in the right places, in financial management," Brad remembers.

The new CFO brought in a new assistant treasurer from one of the banks, and Brad got the boot. "He argued that this guy knows what the lenders are thinking," says Brad. So having a mentor, even at the very top of the organization, doesn't always help you to survive.

However, it did help Brad get an extremely generous severance package, and it also helped him get another job. "I'm one of the few who got out and was treated very well. I went from assistant treasurer to VP of finance at another company, in real estate. I changed industries and moved up the ladder at the same time."

The conclusion here is that finding a mentor might not help you to hang onto your job in the taken-over company, but it might be enormously useful in securing a good severance package and getting resituated.

Getting Your Opponent to Fall on His Own Knife

"The second most common type of backstabbing is when collaborators get in a horse race," says consultant Lind. This is part of the dreadful game of musical chairs that is so often played after the takeover. One way to backstab is to discredit the other person. The previous example was an illustration of this. But there's another way to backstab: Exclude your opponent from meetings by not telling him, or by scheduling the meetings when he's out of town, or by forgetting to send him a memo announcing the meeting.

This happened to Ben, 36, an assistant VP in a financial services company recently taken over by a New York conglomerate. He and his rival, Richard, also 36, reported to different executives, but both were put in charge of getting a new project rolling which the parent company is interested in. On this project, they both reported to the new chairman of the financial services outfit, who recently was brought in by the new parent.

Richard acted as an obstructionist, making plans without taking Ben into account, although they had previously agreed he would be involved in the planning. He did all the things mentioned—neglected to send memos, scheduled meetings when Ben was out of town, the works.

Ben, however, retaliated. First, he told his boss that this behavior was dangerous to the boss. Second, he arranged meetings where other high-level people would hear about the project. Ben arranged the agenda so that the top brass would know he'd been excluded. He held these progress meetings when all senior executives were present. Then he said there were gaps in his knowledge. This forced Richard to jump in and say, "Oh, we've handled that." But this project was important to the parent company, and senior people started coming up to Ben and saying, "I don't know how you can handle this and still put up with this sort of thing."

Ben's strategy paid off. The chairman cashiered Richard and put the whole project under Ben's control. Ben was lucky. The chairman could just as easily have decided he didn't want either of these guys wasting his time. But this is the way it is with knife fights—they can be dangerous.

KEY POINTS

- Be careful before you mark someone as a backstabber. Some of what appears to be backstabbing may not be.
- In order to appear to be good guys and keep their knives from glimmering in the sunlight, cutthroat executives sometimes use the strategy of "going by the book."
- Managers whose indispensability comes from knowing where the bodies are buried are often cut down to size rather than fired. They should use their knowledge to gain time to find another job.
- Losing your mentor can leave you vulnerable to any cheap corporate punk with a penknife. Your best defense is to find another mentor fast.
- When a rival cuts you out of key information, you *can* cut him back. But be forewarned: Knife fighting is dangerous, and although top management may like your spunk, it may decide not to keep *any* barroom brawlers on staff.

THE EIGHTH ORDEAL
The Handwriting on the Wall

Overcoming Denial

"If I knew how to help people overcome denial, I'd deserve the Nobel Prize," says Mitchell Levitt, president of Klein Behavioral Science Consultants of New York. He's not kidding. Talk to any consultant who has advised on the staffing issues in takeovers and any manager who has lived through a takeover, and one term will inevitably come up: *denial*. This is the belief that the next person will get fired, not you. This occurs despite the overwhelming evidence that your company, division, unit, or you are on the scrap heap. So you stay until it's too late.

Denial, says Levitt, "is the process of distorting for emotional reasons the objective facts of the circumstances in which you find yourself." So either you don't see the handwriting on the wall, or if you do, you think it spells out some other guy's name.

The corporate set-up works against having a realistic analysis of the situation. Pensions, by and large, aren't portable. So we want to stay until vested, and we have an incentive to distort facts that might make us realize that we can't stay. We're also caught by our possessions. If a lot of people are fired at the same time, the local housing market may become glutted. So the guy who is forced to sell his house can get a second kick in the groin. There are emotional traps, too. People get comfortable. In fact, getting comfortable may have been the reason they got into the corporate set-up in the first place. Now they don't want to think about change, which inevitably means getting less comfortable.

If you can break out of the denial trap, you can see the handwriting on the wall. Who wants to see that graffiti? You do, if you want to beat the housing market glut and get a jump on the job market. The advantages of getting the message and getting out before what you thought was *your* company axes you are overwhelming.

If you can get a new job while you still have your old one, you're in a better bargaining position for everything from salary to title to relocation expenses. You will also have the extraordinary cachet of being one of the employed when so many others are cut down. People who are fired, almost regardless of the reason, are stigmatized in this country. The assumption is nearly automatic that something is wrong with them and that the full story is not being told on why they were fired. Here's the party line on fired managers: "There's usually a personality problem or clash which they don't like to talk about." Legions of headhunters, consultants, and job counselors will tell you one version or another of this remark. If it's true, then American managers suffer personality problems in distressingly disproportionate numbers.

Outplacement tends to reinforce this interpretation of the inferiority of the fired. What's the first thing that typically happens when someone enters outplacement? He or she is given a battery of psychological tests, ostensibly to help in job counseling. But for the person who feels insecure and hurt from being fired, the tests may seem painfully like diagnostic tests to determine the nature of his illness. What might he be sick from? Maybe his office was on the wrong floor when the company was taken over.

These days, people who've been fired should not automatically be lumped in with the unfit. But many headhunters do, avoiding managers in outplacement, no matter how good they are, in favor of those who are holding down jobs, no matter how mediocre they may be. For the headhunters, the already employed are simply an easier sell. This is because the fired are treated by many, but not all, as if they carry the plague of failure. By contrast, the employed are treated by nearly everyone as if they radiate with the glow of employment fitness. The fact that they are holding down a job is proof that they are fit. Is this prejudice against the fired idiotic? You bet it is, but it's also true. So you really do need to break out of denial.

"Denial takes place," says Levitt, "because there's never another voice besides your own." You repeat "the facts" to yourself or

The Handwriting on the Wall

talk them over with others such as colleagues or a spouse who are also caught up in the turmoil. Nobody has an objective view.

The only way to break out of denial is to get another voice going on the problem. Levitt advises bringing in a third party—a semiretired mentor, somebody you have lunch with once or twice a week, a close friend, or a person in another division of your company. Then simply describe in minute detail what's going on. But don't ask for advice. Ask this third party to simply repeat back to you what you've said. "Let me tell you what you've told me"—that's what he should say and do. Your chance at objectivity comes from his "reflecting back," to use Levitt's term, what you've told him. "There's something dramatic about hearing the words from another person," says Levitt.

It might not sound like much, but it could save your career.

Learning to Read the Graffiti

The manager enjoying his blissful denial may very well sleepwalk right into a brick wall. The alert manager, by contrast, not only avoids walking into the wall, but is constantly reading the graffiti written on it. Sometimes he spots his own name, crossed out.

Several of the people whose stories have been told in this book did not get caught up in denial, spotted the handwriting on the wall, and acted appropriately. The trick is to be sensitive to the behavior patterns of those around you and to know whether you are getting the short end of the stick. What follows is a description of subtle and not-so-subtle messages that may all mean the same thing: You're about to be fired.

Short Change

When a local commercial bank was acquired by a large regional one, the managers in the acquired bank suddenly noticed that they were getting all the lousy loan applications—the most difficult to analyze and the riskiest for the officer authorizing them. Although the loans were all regional, the officers began to feel they were on the Brazil desk. By contrast, the managers from the acquiring bank were getting the safer, smoother loans, the ones that were easier to analyze and less likely to blow up later.

Three of these short-changed managers cottoned on and got out. One left banking altogether, a second made a lateral move, but the third jumped up to become the senior manager of commercial lending in a larger bank. "I wouldn't have moved except that I felt I was being maneuvered into a position where my performance simply couldn't shine," he said later.

Leveling

In some mergers, there will be two line VPs for each major division. Many top managers solve the problem by firing one. But others want to keep both. They rarely make them co-equals, which means that one, usually from the acquirer, becomes the boss of the other. This is tough on the new underling because he used to be at the top himself. "The new top guy has to understand the other and vice versa," says Boston management consultant Peter B. Olney, adding, "they have to sit down and level with each other."

If the new boss doesn't do this leveling, the relationship might not work out, and ultimately both managers could get blamed. Both could get fired too, although the top man might be able to slither out of it by passing the blame below. So one critical piece of graffiti to watch out for is any sign that your boss is screwing up in such a way that you could take the rap—whether or not he gets shafted too.

Gladhanding

"When people you are not normally friendly with suddenly get friendly, get nervous," advises John P. Sullivan of Management Campus, Inc., Atlanta consultants. An example of this happened to a VP of marketing at a Fortune 500 transportation company. A takeover had brought in a new controller who, as these things usually go after takeovers, was trying to cut back on cash expenses to pay off debt. Naturally, this put him at loggerheads with the marketing man. The two had words on more than one occasion. Then, suddenly, the controller became friendly and the marketing man thought he was making progress. And he was—toward the street. He was fired shortly afterwards. "The controller knew I wouldn't be around, so he wanted to keep the waters warm," said the displaced marketing man.

Craving Your Wisdom

What applies to newfound friends goes doubly for newly arriving consultants. If they become great fans of your judgment and information, get your resumé in circulation, fast. "Instead, some people get flattered," says Sullivan. Then they get the shaft.

An example was the VP of organizational planning at a major

consumer goods company. He was virtually adopted by an outside consultant, who pumped him for his ideas and evaluations of people, programs, policies, and markets. Six months later he was called in to his boss's office, and as he put it, encouraged "to seek alternative possibilities."

According to a number of consultants, this happens quite frequently. In fact, a lot of executives hire consultants to do dirty jobs they feel squeamish about doing themselves. The consultant can become even more than a crutch, he can, in effect, be the hidden head of the company. However, this can be his undoing as far as snookering you is concerned. This consultant did not come from the moon. Find out where he's been before, find someone who knew him there, and get the scoop. Some consultants have reputations for being hatchet men.

No Stay Bonus

If you're toward the top, the new management may offer you a special payment to stay, appropriately called a "stay bonus." "Often it's a week's pay for each month you stay on for the next six months," says Peter Krist, a human resources consultant based in Greenwich, Connecticut, and former senior VP at the Mobil Oil Corporation. If you don't get a stay bonus, you might start wondering. However, this isn't a sure sign. "It doesn't necessarily follow every time that if you don't get a stay bonus you're marked to go," cautions Krist, whose advice is to "look at the whole mosaic—including who the new owners are." This, of course, is always critical.

Stay bonuses sometimes confirm the trickle-down theory of wealth distribution. If your boss gets one, he might go back to top management and explain that if he is to keep his own key people he'll have to start divvying out the cash as well. But top management might only let him pass out a couple of these bundles. So if you find that your boss got one and one or two of your peers did as well, but you didn't, the handwriting may be staring you in the face.

Sleeping Bosses

"If top management has been viewed as sleeping at the switch," says Krist, "this will also be viewed as evidence of incompetence below them." In other words, if the division has been run incompetently and has been losing money, senior management will of course be blamed. But the next question the new owners will ask is, "What about the people working for those nincompoops? Why did they stick around?" There may be a variety of good reasons, but the new owners are unlikely to want to hear them. "Birds of a feather" will be the explanation they will most likely leap to, adding, "The kind of managers we want wouldn't put up with lousy bosses for one minute." Then they will fire everyone in sight. It may not be fair, but it's probably what will happen. It is usually referred to as "cleaning house," and several examples in other chapters of this book have illustrated the wholesale slaughter that accompanies this attitude of new management.

Dead Silence

As we've seen in several examples discussed in this book, mergers are usually accompanied by a statement from the top saying what the new management plans to do. Typically management announces that it doesn't plan to do anything for a while. As we've seen, the statement is nearly always false, either because top management doesn't know what it's doing or because it *does* know. Normally these announcements are true to the extent that it takes top management a month or two to figure out what's what. But sometimes they know precisely what they want to do before they close the deal. "If there's dead silence, nothing in the press, it's time to worry," cautions Krist.

An example of this happened when the owner of a West Coast mail order seed business bought one on the East Coast. The East Coast seed company's nurseries were situated on land bought 50 years earlier when it was out in the country. Now it was on the outskirts of a major city. The acquirer said nothing when he bought the company, and the managers at the acquired company were puzzled by the silence. One VP suspected the worst and quit for another job immediately. The others held on, assuming the new owner was simply the closed-mouth type, but good-hearted, like Gary Cooper. But he turned out to be more like Clint Eastwood facing managers who were trying to make his day. He sold the land at once, which paid for the acquisition. Then he closed out the East Coast headquarters, firing everyone who worked there, and leased additional land to meet the mail order demands of his newly acquired customers. So if what you hear is silence, you may have an asset stripper on your hands.

Denied Expense Reports

"If a $120 dinner suddenly becomes too expensive to be approved, even though you've been charging that same type of expense for years, watch out," warns Richard B. Warren, the president of Cole, Warren and Long Inc., Philadelphia consultants. An extreme example happened to the director of personnel for a Maryland insurance company. For the previous seven years he had taken new VP candidates and their wives to dinner if they made it to the second interview. He viewed this as valuable public relations, and his own boss not only agreed but strongly encouraged it. However, the personnel director was transferred to a new boss as a result of a corporate restructuring after the company was sold by one conglomerate to another. And the new boss didn't want to spend any discretionary money on recruitment. Unfortunately, he neglected to tell this to the personnel man, who was called on the carpet for one of these dinners and then fired for it.

Of course, there was no handwriting on the wall in this case, so the key is to search out this sort of information whenever you get a new boss, but before you spend any discretionary money.

Downgraded Security Clearances

"If you work in a company which gets security clearances for its employees," says Warren, who consults for many such companies, "and your security clearance is suddenly downgraded so that you don't get documents on a need-to-know basis, figure someone higher up has decided you'll be gone within six months." This happened to a man in R&D who had been part of a team designing a new integrated circuit. "Suddenly I found I wasn't invited to the meetings and therefore wasn't shown the documents as a consequence of the meetings," he reported. A few months later he got the bad news.

Nixed Privileges and Perks

Some companies issue plastic cards to get into the managers' parking lot. For a variety of reasons, they are routinely collected and replaced. If yours is collected, but not replaced, assume the worst. This happened to 200 managers at a major West Coast aerospace company. When one asked his boss where his new card was, the boss replied, "Gee, I don't know why you didn't get it, let me check into it." Two weeks later he still hadn't quite gotten around to finding out the reason. "You can always park in the worker's lot," he said defensively. One month after this conversation, all 200 were fired.

The parking lot is only one giveaway that something is up. There are other losses of executive privileges, reported by a number of managers and consultants, which work the same way, for example, booking tables in the top executives' dining room or meetings in the board room. The CEO's secretary often keeps the booking log for the board room. If she suddenly says you need your boss's approval to book it when you hadn't needed it before, watch out.

This can be a particularly insidious piece of handwriting on the wall, because it can hit you at the very last minute, when you are trying to keep up a positive front. "I've been in meetings where the guy said we'd meet in the board room. Then he came back and said we'd have to meet somewhere else," reported Richard Warren, who added, "We knew he was on his way out, but he didn't. He was just pissed because he couldn't get the room." This was a clear case of denial.

A Boss Who Acts Like James Bond

If your boss appears to be working with new people and is acting mysterious about it, be warned. For example, a manager in a large service organization asked his boss what had happened at an unscheduled meeting out of town. The boss replied, "Oh, not much, don't worry about it. I can't talk about it." A few months later the inquiring manager had a lot of time on his hands to reflect on this encounter.

If you're having drinks over at your boss's place and the doorbell rings, interrupting the party, you might not think anything of it. But if you look out the window and see that a messenger wearing a Burberry raincoat hands your boss a plain brown envelope with no return address but only the words "Project Blue Sky" written on it, be careful. Either (1) your boss works for Colonel Oliver North, or (2) the company is about to move its corporate headquarters, which frequently happens after takeovers. Consultants who specialize in corporate moving sometimes communicate their reports to top brass in precisely this cloak and dagger manner. The documents never pass through the hands of the secretaries and in fact are usually hand-delivered to the CEO's home. Of course, a corporate move may mean a restructuring, and it may be the first vague bit of graffiti indicating that you could be marked.

Postponement of Performance Appraisal Without Good Reason

Suppose you get a great performance appraisal, describing in superlative language how much of a contribution to the company you have been making and saying, correctly, what a great guy you are. It does what performance appraisals are supposed to do—details specific projects on which you've worked and describes your very real accomplishments. This document makes it psychologically tough for your boss to fire you the next day, which is what his boss might ask him to do. It also could be an interesting paper to show the jury in the event you decide to sue the collective pants off the corporation.

"By postponing the performance review, there is nothing in the manager's file or in the boss's conscience that says anything good about the manager, so they don't have to countermand a positive performance appraisal," says Larry Axline, the 46-year-old president of Management Action Planning Inc., consultants, of Boulder, Colorado. This postponement happened to the chief financial officer of a Western financial services company. He had always received very good performance evaluations, and deservedly so. Not only had he been an outstanding credit administrator, approving only the best loans and not taking any dangerous ones, but he had also been an outstanding person to work for. A true mentor to his trusted subordinates, he had personally seen to their rapid advancement.

In fact, his subordinates had progressed so rapidly under the able guidance of the CFO that the company no longer needed the boss. In addition, the CEO had changed the policies, allowing riskier credit. But the CFO didn't fully agree with the new policies, and was thus held to be too rigid and inflexible. His attitude made him of little help in dealing with the new kind of customers the CEO wanted to go after—the ones who pay near loan-shark rates because they're bad credit risks. So, his performance appraisal was withheld. How could the CEO do otherwise? He couldn't very well write down "too much integrity," and "champion of those who work for him, whom he trains outstandingly." The delay in the performance appraisal made the CFO sweat, but not for long. Thirty days later, he was fired.

Perception That No One Cares

"When no one seems to care how you spend your time," warns Axline, "and you're not accountable to anyone and [are] becoming even less so, you should be concerned." After all, who's going to stick up for you in the event of a retrenchment? If no one [else] needs you, why should the company? This is a common problem for in-house staff attorneys and accountants, who function without attachment to anyone. They can suddenly find themselves very much unattached.

Indifference to you no matter what you do can also happen when your mentor gets fired or jumps ship, which is what happened to Gus, 48, the divisional manager of manufacturing for the international operations of a major package goods company, which was itself gobbling up other companies. He had held the job for three years of solid achievement, continual pay raises, and kudos from the CEO. He had every reason to believe that his future looked golden. Then his boss and mentor got into an argument with the CEO. "There's never any doubt who wins those," said Gus.

His boss had refused to take the fall over an acquisition the CEO had made in Europe that had gone sour. Without a mentor, Gus decided his only chance was take on more work and try to make himself indispensable. In addition to his current job, he took charge of the food services products division, which didn't have a manager at the time because of retrenchments due to losses on the European operation. But the added responsibilities didn't seem to improve his prospects. "Two months later, I was told I should look elsewhere while I continued on salary for a couple of months," reported Gus.

But instead of searching for another job, Gus doubled his efforts at his current one, still hoping to make a good impression. Gus knew that another senior manager was about to retire, so there might still be room for him. "I figured they'd slot me in there," said Gus. But nobody, including the CEO, cared about his overwhelming efforts. "When they play taps, it's over," concluded Gus.

Here's the key question to ask yourself when you see indifference to your efforts, no matter how good they are: Do I any longer have powerful sponsors or supporters in this organization? If the answer is no, the handwriting is on the wall.

Assignment to Community Service

"Some companies provide loaned executives to community service; it means that this is an executive they can spare, regardless of the honorable intentions of the company," says Calvin K. Sholl, chairman of Boston consultants Parker, Sholl and Gordon Inc. For example, a founding partner in a very large CPA firm had not been serving clients directly for some time. He didn't want retraining and his partners didn't want to retrain him. However, to avoid a stink, the partners wanted to ease him out in a way that didn't strip him of his dignity. Since he clearly wasn't profitable for the firm, they moved him into the nonprofit area—public service. This sort of thing can have as much to do with performance as with a merger. But if a merger or retrenchment occurs while you're out there serving the public, you might find yourself left out there with the public.

Even if you aren't loaned out, assignments to highly visible external affairs projects can also be giveaways that you don't count for much, especially if the projects cost the company lots of money. Usually the people who count in companies, especially during times of retrenchment, are those who bring the money in, not those who dish it out. It may mean you are dispensable if a future staff cutback becomes necessary. This happened to a senior VP at a major corporation who was in charge of giving away money to worthy causes. When his own company went through a retrenchment, he found that he *himself* was a worthy cause.

When a Nice Boss Turns Nasty

"If your relationship with your boss has been good, but suddenly becomes less good, be wary," warns Sholl. Your boss may be under pressure to dump you but may have to readjust psychologically to work himself up to the hatchet job. Also, maybe he hopes that if he's nasty you'll wise up and run, so he won't have to kick you out. The sudden nastiness can take many forms. One is a general insensitivity on the part of upper management in the hope that you'll take the hint. Another is carping criticism of everything you do. For years, you may have been presenting your views at operational review meetings to a favorable response. All of a sudden the meetings become vicious, as people begin to attack you and you're picked apart. Incidentally, not only the boss, but his secretary may suddenly be rude to you. All of these unpleasant experiences could be taken as evidence that you have been the subject of a previous discussion.

Finding Yourself Out of the Loop

Ask any consultant what is the main graffiti on the wall, and the odds are he'll mention this as the major sign to watch out for. You used to be invited to meetings, but suddenly you aren't, or maybe you were included routinely on certain memo distributions, but suddenly you're not. This happened to Helen, 51, head of management information services for a manufacturing company with $350 million in sales. The company was going through some legal maneuverings. Although she had dutifully gone along with them in a written memo, she had expressed her verbal objections to the CEO. In this company, even a hint of loyal disagreement was enough to mark someone as a potential troublemaker.

As the company geared up to move its corporate headquarters from New York to Texas, Helen found that she was undergoing a change in status. She had always been routinely present at key meetings and often prepared the agendas for them. Typically, she would send the CEO a memo on some point that she thought needed discussion, and he would photocopy and distribute it as the agenda, adding at the bottom a routine list of who was to be present. Then, after her verbal objection to the legal maneuver, she found her name no longer listed as part of the routine group, but as a "guest" at the meeting. As she sat at the meeting, she realized that there had been other meetings on the subject to which she had not been invited. She was out of the loop. She later found out that the comptroller had proposed to the CEO that Helen's job be cut, and he would take over MIS, thus saving the company her $85,000 salary.

Finding Your Office Relocated

If you or your department is moved in any unfavorable way, watch out. Usually, if you're moved farther from the CEO, you're moving in the wrong direction. Perhaps this idea comes from Louis XIV, who assembled all the noblemen in Versailles so he could keep his eye on them. If the boss no longer wants you as close as he once did, perhaps he doesn't think you're as potentially dangerous as he once did. So you must have slipped in his esteem.

Alternatively, the boss may make you more visible not only to himself, but to everyone else as well. This happened to Kevin, 52, an associate administrator of a hospital that had just merged with another. The merger left the hospital with twice as big a staff as it needed, so quite a few managers got marked for the ax, including Kevin. However, he had a powerful friend on the board of directors, which meant no one had the guts even to tip Kevin off that the new bosses wanted to fire him, but couldn't figure out a graceful way to do it. However, they felt perfectly at ease letting him know that he was no longer wanted. This they tried to do by literally moving him, his desk, his phone, and his wastebasket out of his office and into the hallway in front of it. The ostensible reason was to repair his office. After three weeks had passed and no repair work was done, but a lot of people had walked by smirking and no work was assigned to him, he was called in by the human resources executive and asked what he thought was going on. "I don't know," he said. The human resources man then broke the bad news, suggesting that Kevin resign on his own, which he did.

He Who Lives by the Sword

Ask any consultant familiar with mergers how hatchet men make out and you might get a surprising answer. Apparently they get fired with amazing consistency. The reason is that they've made so many enemies that they're no longer useful. Also, getting rid of them can be a way for top management to signal that the purges are over. So one question to ask yourself is whether you've become a hatchet man. If so, your name may be the last one scribbled on the wall.

Following a takeover, a new CEO, 49, took charge of a major national department store chain. He decided to reorient the chain to the youth market, so his first order of business was to ax everyone over 50 that he could. The policy, of course, was illegal, in clear violation of federal law, but incidents of this kind had not yet made the headlines in any celebrated cases.

To carry out this illegal policy, the CEO needed an accomplice, which he found in the existing VP of personnel, who was himself in his mid-50s, but was assured that he was one of the "good" over-50s. He started rumors, which were true, about the new direction of the company. A few of the over-50 crowd left on their own. Then he encouraged younger people to lodge complaints against older ones. More left. He even got younger people to come into the stores and complain about the older sales people. By this time, a lot of the older crowd got fed up and left, and some of the others were fired on trumped-up complaints.

Many of these people had friends who were still on the payroll. To placate the angered remaining employees, the new CEO fired the VP of personnel. Robespierre went to the guillotine too. This is what usually seems to happen to hatchet men, who in effect write their own names on the wall.

In this particular case, however, the CEO put his smoking gun in his pants pocket and it accidentally went off. The VP of personnel took all the documentation for what happened with him, and he sued. The parent company then fired the CEO and settled out of court with the VP for a reputed $300,000. Incidentally, this hatchet man, either to atone for or compound his wicked past, went on to become an executive recruiter.

How to Spot the Graffiti in a Phony Retention Interview

Your last shot at hanging on may be at the retention interview. This is when one of the new bosses arrives and interviews you for a possible job in the new set-up. The chapter on selling yourself gave some pointers on how to do well in these things. Not every acquiring company uses retention interviews. For example, if everyone is going to be fired they may not bother.

But even with those companies that do use them, these interviews may be conducted as much to head off future lawsuits as they are to select people to retain. What kinds of lawsuits? Age discrimination suits for one. Either it is a bizarre accident that outplacement offices are "seas of grey hair," as New York outplacement consultant Jay Bushell has described them, or there is massive age discrimination taking place. But company executives can't come out and say, "We've decided to fire everyone over 50." Not unless they want every contingency lawyer in the country hanging out in the parking lot. Instead, managers are put through a "retention" interview, which is proof that the new owners gave them all a fair chance and also documents the exact question to which the manager failed to give the correct answer. As luck would have it, it just so happens that those over 50 don't seem to do well in these retention interviews.

Occasionally, the interviewer botches the job so badly that the fact of prejudgment becomes obvious. According to a number of consultants, there are obvious signs of phoniness, which can reveal the insincerity of the interviewer. All of them come down to the same thing—the interviewer doesn't give a damn what the "candidate" says. These interviews, therefore, offer more graffiti signs to which you should be alerted. Here are a few of the more notorious ones: If the interviewer cuts you short, or doesn't write down or record your answers in any way, be suspicious. If he fails to ask any follow-up questions which carry forward a line of thought, you also have a pretty good idea of what's going on. Another thing to look for is if the interviewer is being particularly concrete about what he's asking. This could mean he's thinking about a specific job he's supposed to fill. If he's very vague, there may be no job at all for anyone on the other side of this interview.

Those are graffiti signs you can watch for. But some graffiti can only be seen when the light shines from the right angle, so it's up to you to bring along a flashlight. According to G. Arthur Black, head of the Pace Services Group, consultants in Suffield, Connecticut, there are a few questions for which a questionable questioner on the other side of the table won't have an answer:

May I see a copy of the organization chart? If the interview is a hoax, there won't be one. However, if there isn't one, that doesn't necessarily mean the interview is a hoax. They may simply be disorganized.

May I see a copy of the position description? If he doesn't have this, forget him and the job.

What are the company goals for that department? If he doesn't know, how does he know whom to look for?

What are the overall company goals? If he again doesn't know, the goal may be asset stripping.

What are my manager and associates like? If he doesn't want to tell you, there may not be any.

What might my career path be with this company? If he says the path leads to the door, you've stopped wasting your time.

All of these are perfectly legitimate questions that a good candidate should ask. And any one of them might shine light on the handwriting on the wall.

If you can spot the handwriting on the wall and get out before you're fired, you can beat the takeover gang at their own game and come out ahead. In the last chapter, "On the Street," we'll help you explore the options once you're out of the company—either by the new bosses' boot or with your own walking shoes.

KEY POINTS

- Denial is one of the toughest things to overcome, but the consequences may be catastrophic if you don't. One way to beat it is to get a friend to reflect back at you exactly what you've described to him or her so you can hear your thoughts in someone else's voice.

- There are a number of clear signs that you're about to be fired detailed in this chapter. They include such widely diverse signals as people suddenly craving your wisdom or becoming utterly indifferent to you. The most common sign is being left out of the loop.

- Retention interviews contain their own specialized graffiti to watch out for. There are special questions you can ask which will make latent signs visible.

THE NINTH ORDEAL
The Breakdown of Loyalty

"Most managers saw through loyalty a long time ago," the career counselor and former head of personnel for a major corporation said, adding, "Over the last ten years, company loyalty [hasn't meant] you'd receive any rewards."

Maybe so, but quite a few managers keep saying how surprised they are when, after years of loyal service to their firm, they get kicked in the face by the firm. So when the takeover finally happens and if the worst fears are confirmed, your ignored, undiscussed, or even suppressed doubts about loyalty will suddenly surface. "The main result of Tisch's taking control of CBS," said a CBS news producer laid off afterwards, "is a breakdown in loyalty. The next place I go I'm not going to trust the organization to reward my loyalty."

When bumped managers move to new jobs and tell their friends about their feelings of having been betrayed, the word soon gets around that you can't count on your company for a steady paycheck. Here is one ordeal of the takeover that doesn't seem to end. This chapter will show why.

The first thing we need to note is the survey evidence to show that the word on loyalty is indeed getting around.

In 1986, *Business Week* arranged for Louis Harris and Associates to poll 600 middle managers, to assess their sense of loyalty to their companies. The conclusions were striking. Although a majority had assumed, when they started their current jobs, that they could stay as long as they did well, less than a majority still thought that was the case after they had been on the job for awhile. Sixty-five percent thought that salaried employees are less loyal to their employers now than they were ten years ago.

The decline in loyalty goes all the way to the top, as revealed in another survey, taken in 1984 by the international executive recruiting firm of Heidrick and Struggles, Inc., headquartered in Chicago. Heidrick and Struggles sent questionnaires to nearly 1600 executives whose names had been mentioned in the "Who's News" column of *The Wall Street Journal*. This column covers the changes in top management in publicly traded Fortune 500 companies and in privately held companies which are at least as big as the 500th on the Fortune list. A little more than a third of these people sent the questionnaires back. So there is a high degree of self-selection in the responses, which is true of most surveys conducted by companies not in the survey business. However, the results were so startlingly in the direction of lack of loyalty that one wonders if those who did not reply simply didn't want to put their true feelings in writing—even anonymously.

The Heidrick and Struggles survey gave eight different definitions of corporate loyalty and allowed each of the executives a chance to be counted under the one that best described himself. Definitions included supporting/being committed to corporate goals, strategies, philosophies, and policies; putting shareholders' interests above all others; being a team player/supporting team effort; placing corporate objectives ahead of personal gain.

Here's the bottom line on the survey:

> The increasing frequency of corporate mergers and takeovers and the cost cutting that is leading to the elimination of executive positions are affecting how mobile managers define corporate loyalty. Traditional views are being questioned, especially among the under-40 age group. Only one third of the respondents define corporate loyalty as support and commitment to corporate goals and strategies, and just slightly more than 11 percent place corporate objectives ahead of personal gain.

The "me first" attitude exhibited in the survey by our corporate role models really gets rolling when the corporate jets they command get shot down by Boesky and others. The top brass rarely go down in flames with their crippled jets. On the contrary, they are

The Breakdown of Loyalty

often the first to bail out since they brought on board their own personal "golden parachutes." If this leaves the rest of the crew to be splattered over the fields below, so be it.

These golden parachute payouts aren't small change. In 1986, according to a survey by New-York-based executive recruiter Gilbert E. Dwyer, who has been tracking them over several years, they varied between $100,000 and $60 million. Recall the changes at CBS discussed in the chapter on rumors. Hundreds of loyal newspeople were ruthlessly kicked out. Those changes came after Thomas H. Wyman was booted out as CEO in a takeover that put Laurence A. Tisch in the control room. But Wyman did not leave empty-handed. He got $4.3 million up front, plus $400,000 each year for life—which may be a long time, since he's only 57—and stock options for amounts the company has not disclosed. And this was for a man whose management judgment had been called into question by more than one analyst.

Imagine the impact of this sort of payment on middle managers who get bumped in the takeovers. They are out on the street scrambling to survive while the top managers whose business judgments may have helped put them there collect bags of cash. This discrepancy in treatment must surely rub salt into the wounds left by the sense of betrayal, and it helps to turn the breakdown in loyalty into a seething cauldron of resentment.

There may be a great deal to be resentful about. According to the Dwyer surveys, not many people are covered by golden parachutes. In 1986, 26 percent covered only the top man. Another 37 percent covered as many as the top five people. A further 30 percent covered up to 24 people, and more than 25 people were covered in less than 9 percent of these contracts. So within each company, not many people get the bailout gold.

However, nearly everywhere you look the top people are making out just fine. By the end of 1986, the total of Fortune 1000 companies with these payouts had gone to 54 percent, up from 49 percent three years earlier.

How big a ground-to-air weapon is required to get the parachute wearers to jump? In some cases, the waving of a cap gun seems to be sufficient. In 1986, 67 percent of these deals allowed the top brass to jump if a change-of-control provision was triggered. This could involve such things as a change in the percentage of ownership by specified stockholders, the loss of a majority of people on the board who support the top managers, or a merger in which the manager's company doesn't come out on top. In other words, the manager doesn't have to be fired; he can simply decide he doesn't like the place anymore. Incidentally, the amount of stock ownership required to signify a change of control doesn't have to be more than 50 percent. In nearly 70 percent of these deals, a 20 percent stake by a new owner will do the trick.

During the takeover, middle managers who suddenly see that the boss will come out fine but they themselves might not, might ask themselves, "Why should I be loyal to this company when the top people don't have to be?" "If only top management people are covered, and others are left without any reasonable protection, the risk of disenchantment is pretty high," said Gilbert Dwyer in an interview. He added, "But most well-managed companies that provide golden parachutes will also provide appropriate protection on a graduated basis for employees at lower salary levels. But there are some companies where the top people take care of themselves and forget about everybody else."

Perhaps for this reason, management has come up with a "tin parachute" for the rest of the crew. The catch is that the crew only gets it in the event of a *hostile* takeover. If the golden parachuted captain of the corporate plane is happy with the corporate skyjacker's terms, the captain bails out and leaves the crew to the sadistic pleasures of the corporate skyjackers. Typical of these tin parachutes are the ones Mobil instituted, which cover 37,000 employees. The usual severance deal at Mobil is to count up one's years on the payroll and multiply that number by two weeks' pay. The tin parachute simply doubles this figure. For the top 800 executives, the tin is shinier—two years of their base pay and a bonus to boot.

But remember, all of this tin gets pocketed by the corporate skyjacker if the takeover is friendly. So the tin parachute has very little to do with helping middle and lower management but a great deal to do with scaring off potential raiders. The message from the captains of industry to the corporate skyjackers is clear: "If you try to board this plane without my permission, I'll see to it that the crew is treated with a modicum of decency, even given a chance to live, and you'll pay for it. See how you like that! But if you're reasonable and come to terms, you may throw them out the cargo hatch at your pleasure and convenience."

What sort of severance deal do most managers get in these situations? In Management Assistance, Inc., a computer company taken over by Asher Edelman in 1985, most managers got two weeks' pay for every year of service to a maximum of twenty-four weeks plus benefits. This was reported by Horace Scharges, the former VP of human resources at the company who helped negotiate the terms with Edelman. The ten top managers made out a bit better, the lower tier of them walking away with two years of salary and benefits plus whatever stock options they had.

Scharges described this as a better deal than many other bumped managers got at other companies, and he was right. For example, when International Harvester sold its farm equipment business to a division of Tenneco in 1985, it also harvested the careers of 400 upper and middle managers with salaries ranging from $25,000 to $80,000 per year. As at Scharges' old company, they got two weeks' pay for every year on the job, but, unlike at Scharges' company, only to a grand total of twelve weeks' pay. The company also threw in a lump sum payment based on grade level, which could go as high as an additional six weeks' pay. Almost everyone got another four weeks of vacation pay. No matter how you cut it, the raider, in this case, paid out a bit more than the old-line company did. Harvester also continued to pay medical and life insurance for a full year after the last day on the job. Edelman was not as generous as the Ford Motor Company when it closed its assembly plant near San Jose, California, in 1983. Every salaried person who had worked for Ford at least a year got two months' pay. Then, for each year up to nine, Ford shelled out an additional half-month's pay. Salaried workers with more than ten years with Ford picked up twenty months of pay, doled out over forty months, however.

The International Harvester and Ford situations are typical examples contained in a survey on business shutdowns by the Conference Board, a nonprofit business information and research organization. Over 60 percent of the 224 companies surveyed offered one form or another of outplacement counseling. Sometimes this was done inhouse, sometimes through one of the professional outplacement firms.

What sort of loyalty do bumped employees feel toward their old companies? The Conference Board survey doesn't say, but there are survey data available on the issue. The study in question focused on the semiconductor industry in Silicon Valley. The sample was small (40), but it was scientifically conducted and the results were interesting. For openers, more than half reported having been led down the garden path by their former bosses and told their jobs were secure shortly before they learned the awful truth. On the other hand, those at the top, defined in this survey as making more than $50,000, tended to be perfectly aware that their jobs weren't secure—after all, the top guys were often privy to the financial facts.

In this survey the key to the survival of a sense of loyalty on the part of those laid off was how many went. If it was a small company and the whole kit and caboodle lost their jobs, including the top people, over 90 percent expressed a sense of commitment to their former company, even though it didn't exist anymore. Essentially, these people didn't feel betrayed. But those laid off by large companies that continued without them did express a sense of betrayal. Seventy percent said the company was not committed to them, even though they had been laid off for economic reasons. Interestingly, 60 percent of these people still expressed a sense of commitment to the company that had tossed them overboard. So there seems to be a residual sense of loyalty even among those who have been treated the worst, which makes one suspect that the raiders may get the last laugh after all. In this context, here's Carl Ichan:

"At TWA—to make it simple, we basically replaced all the top management.... We really replaced the whole 42nd floor. There's nobody there on the 42nd floor at 605 Third Avenue who was there before. Possibly there's one but I think he's leaving. And it had to be done. And not because they're all bad guys and not because they're all incapable. But where there's a bureaucracy, there is a problem."

Why the Loyalty Ordeal Keeps Dogging You

For the manager caught up in the ordeals of the takeover, the problem of loyalty is especially vicious. After the deal is set, his new bosses expect him to show loyalty more than ever. If he doesn't, he could be among the first to be bumped, and it will be much more difficult to be loyal to the next company he moves to. But at the same time, all the forces in the business world are working to make loyalty an utterly irrelevant attitude. In this section of the chapter we'll discuss the forces destroying loyalty, and in the next we'll point out some of the pressures that force managers to pretend to have loyalty.

Corporate loyalty traditionally has involved (1) following the rules, (2) taking orders, (3) trusting the judgments of those who gave them, and (4) being rewarded for doing all of the above. But during takeovers and retrenchments, all of these aspects of loyalty come under tremendous pressure as the manager gets hit in the face by some of the most dynamic forces in the business world. Here are some of these forces.

The Headhunters

Consultants and managers almost universally report that headhunters appear at the first rumor of a takeover or retrenchment. They immediately start enticing people to new, better paying jobs.

The Breakdown of Loyalty

How can you be loyal when your boss, who knows how well you've been doing and therefore could see to it that you get rewarded, has just jumped to a better job somewhere else? There's a bizarre paradox in this. Those involved report that "the best people make out fine" in takeovers, meaning they get lured away to other jobs or get contracts to stay on under favorable terms. Their hand is strengthened in bargaining for these terms because headhunters have offered them alternative jobs. We've looked at several examples in earlier chapters. So "the best people" don't need to show loyalty.

Headhunters are an interesting lot. The fancy ones are paid by retainer from the company doing the looking. The less fancy are paid by commission. The typical retainer is 30 to 33 percent of the annual base salary and cash bonuses paid to the executive delivered, according to Robert Montgomery, 41, the 1987 president of the Association of Executive Search Consultants. This is an association of 70 firms, up from 55 just two years earlier. "The recruiting profession over the past 10 or 15 years has grown dramatically—many more firms that are much more competitive, which forces better quality work," says Montgomery. These are by no means the only firms in the industry. Montgomery estimates the total number of retainer search firms, operating under written contract, at about 1,500.

Even without takeovers and retrenchments, incidentally, some have claimed that these headhunters have undercut loyalty. The claim is that these people make their money the way unscrupulous stockbrokers do—from churning the account. In other words the bum stockbroker gets paid by commission, so keeps buying and selling the client's stocks. The unscrupulous headhunter upsets loyal, stable relationships by luring otherwise satisfied executives away from their firms to those that pay bigger bundles. Other executives are not yet corrupted away, but take one look at the big money and wish they were. As a result, loyalty takes a beating. Is there any truth to this claim?

"The executive search firm has had some impact," concedes Montgomery. "But not as great an impact as one might suspect," he adds. His reason:

> I don't think this is an important part of the weakening of loyalty because of the small chance that a headhunter will call. We aren't in the business of finding jobs for people; we find people for jobs. It's coincidental that an executive happens to be contacted by a headhunter; he can't sit around waiting for a recruiter to phone.

Perhaps, but any number of managers have described swarms of these people hanging around during the takeover and retrenchment.

Montgomery claims the degradation of loyalty is really the corporations' fault:

> The executive search firm has given the employer an alternative he never had. Before, he could only get those on the market. Now executive search firms create a market. We go to persons content and happy until they realize there is an opportunity substantially more exciting.

Bill Gould, 54, a former president of the Association of Executive Search Consultants and the Chairman of Gould & McCoy, Inc., doesn't think the headhunters have played a big part in the decline of loyalty: "In 1986, we as a profession accounted for probably 20 percent of the total executive changes in this country. The other 80 percent were through boards of directors, contacts, and networking. So I don't think we were that big a factor in the overall loyalty equation."

While not arguing that executive recruiters lure somewhat contented people away to bigger pots of gold, Gould does protest that "We don't make that market." He explains: "We are asked to participate by the client, who gives us a very tight specification including salary ranges. This is tied directly to the current competitive factors in the marketplace. We are not trying to lure people away with inflated salary offers."

The Footloose MBAs

These are people in their twenties, with degrees from prestigious schools, who can easily walk away from any job where the boss or the company becomes more trouble than it's worth. And during a takeover, the footloose MBAs often show how mobile they are. Again, they get rewarded for their lack of loyalty, but those who don't have the high-powered credentials and stay may not be viewed as loyal, merely as less mobile.

The footloose MBAs' contribution to the collapse of loyalty usually is alleged to come from two phenomena. One is the MBAs' feeling a stronger commitment to their management profession than to the company. Recall the survey of top management's definition of loyalty. One of the definitions was "Be a team player." It was supported most by those under age 40. The survey doesn't say so, but these supporters are likely, given their standing in the corporate world, to be footloose MBAs. The second phenomenon is the bidding war companies wage for these top MBAs. They often start with a salary of $60,000 per year—for brats who've never worked a day in their lives. Three years later, another company will often hire them out for $120,000. "How can [these people] be loyal?" asks executive search consultant Montgomery.

What do these young MBAs have to do for their $120,000 per year? Plenty. Almost any recruiter, outplacement counselor, or executive you talk to will report the same thing—to earn this kind of money one has to routinely work 80 hours or more a week, seven days a week, and keep it up for three to five years. This often results in burnout.

So the footloose MBA is like a baseball pitcher with only a few good throwing years. He's got to extract the maximum money during those years, and then trade up to a more realistically sustainable pace, involving a better life style, at another company. So disloyalty to the company during the jackhammer years is built into the deal.

Computers

Because of the debt run up in the takeover, payrolls inevitably have to be cut. So the replacement of number-crunching managers by machines, a process that was already under way even without the takeovers, is speeded up. Beyond that, some seemingly highly skilled tasks may soon be computer programmed through the techniques of artificial intelligence. If machinery can substitute for manual labor and tedious clerical work, why not intelligent work? "The craftsmanship of the manager or the professional may be over or at least changed," says New York outplacement counselor Jay Bushell.

Much routine work now done by lawyers and accountants may fall into this category. "The de-skilling of work is going up the corporate ladder," adds Bushell, "especially in areas where pay gets way ahead of that for other occupations." This process will probably destroy whatever residual loyalty the remaining brain workers may have.

Who Wants Loyalty?

As we saw, during the takeover, the headhunters help to dash successful people's loyalty to bits, and the footloose MBAs might not need the headhunters' help. Those ignored by the headhunters and left behind by the footloose MBAs may still exhibit the old loyalty, but who wants it? It may be viewed, if not described, as a bad attitude.

After the takeover, the new owners have taken on huge debt. They need real go-getters to work it off. But loyalty isn't the attitude normally associated with movers and shakers. Rosabeth Moss Kanter, formerly a professor at the Yale Graduate School of Management, has been quoted in *The New York Times* as saying, "The sleepy solid citizen who stays with the company for 30 years isn't loyal, he is simply viewed as having nowhere else to go." In this vein, John Teets, CEO of the Greyhound Corporation, has said, "I want spirited managers who will challenge the system. I don't want lukewarm employees. They breed mediocrity and a womb-to-tomb attitude." Mr. Teets is undoubtedly sincere in his remarks, but what else can a CEO say in public these days? J. Edgar Hoover once said he only hired his FBI agents out of one particular law school because "they take orders and don't think." But this author has never heard a CEO say for attribution, "I want mediocre slugs who toady up to me until they retire or I fire them."

Naturally, there's a pejorative term for one-company, loyal people—"tree huggers." There aren't vast numbers of them anymore. Managers now average 8.8 years at one company. As recently as 1981, the average tenure had been 12 years. According to Spencer Stuart, an executive search firm, if the present trend continues, the average manager will soon work at seven to ten companies during his or her career. In the early 1970s, the comparable figure was three to four companies.

For one-company executives who find their loyalty isn't returned when they get bumped in a retrenchment, the problems are especially tough. Fred Hoag was a manager at IBM, where he had worked for 33 years. Forced into early retirement at age 57, he was quoted in *The Wall Street Journal* as saying, "I knew in the back of my mind years ago that things had leveled off for me and I should get out, but I kept believing the company would take care of me." Then he found out the real shocker. "All the guys who knew my work and might have recommended me for a change are retired now," he said.

In some industries, particularly those in which mergers have been extensive, loyalty can mean only staying at a job for a few years. Advertising is typical. A *New York Times* article on this point quotes Bob Robbins, a VP at the New York agency of Geers Gross. Although only in his thirties, he's in his fifth job. Here's what he says about them: "The common thread through all of my job moves has been that I have left when I felt my skills can no longer be tested. I'm committed to an organization as long as I am challenged."

Loyal to What?

Companies that are using a takeover strategy sometimes change their names. But this can cause loyalty problems since it can finally make both employees and shareholders aware that the company isn't what it used to be. United Airlines, for example, was once a company whose name suggested what business it was in. Then its CEO, Richard J. Ferris, decided on a grand strategy for the company that involved acquisitions of hotel and rental car businesses. As part of this strategy, he changed the name of the company to Allegis Corporation. Not everyone was happy. A major stockholder, Donald Trump, said the name sounded like "the next world class disease." A few weeks after the name change, the board dumped Ferris, replacing him with Frank A. Olsen, who announced he would restore the old name of the company.

According to Clive Chajet, head of the company that dreamed up the new name, the purpose of the new name was to raise the price of the stock by getting securities analysts to realize the company wasn't simply an airline. "The idea was to have the company perceived for what it was. And we succeeded. The stock price just about doubled," said Chajet. However, whatever the company was called, raiders kept offering more than the stock market was paying, so the name couldn't cover up the company's bust-up value.

Concerning another well-known company, Tom Peters has written, "the name change from U.S. Steel to USX simply codified what we all knew. The bloated and drifting firm is no longer a viable steel company; Big Steel restructured itself out of its basic business and it's still losing money." If companies are treated as commodities, or as "hollow shells" that simply jump from business line to business line as seems momentarily convenient, and if the so-called shareholders are really institutional portfolio managers who buy a stock one minute and sell it ten minutes later, neither the companies nor the stockholders can be taken seriously. They may be feared for the damage they can do, but they don't inspire loyalty.

Personal Loyalty Is Hard to Transfer

Much of what passes for loyalty now is not to the firm but to specific individuals in it. Recall the Silicon Valley survey on commitment.

Many of those who still felt committed to their old companies, even after the companies went down the drain, had worked for small companies and had a personal sense of loyalty to the entrepreneurs who had founded them. This was the unique sense of excitement of a small group of people struggling together for the good of all. Many of these companies are privately owned.

Could this kind of personal loyalty be coming back as a result of leveraged buyouts? Maybe, but probably not. The new owners, usually former managers in the company, take on so much debt that they inevitably fire their former colleagues in wholesale lots in order to pay off the debt. This is unlikely to inspire loyalty. Also, quite a few of the new owner-managers plan to resell the company to the public at some later date. The process is not so different from that of new owners buying a rental apartment building for the purpose of co-oping it to the tenants. The tenants' loyalty to the co-oping management corporation may very well be about as strong as that the new leveraged buyout owners can get from their employees.

Although the usual period before the object of a leveraged buyout is resold to the public is five years, several deals have happened much faster. For example, Tiffany and Company, the famous jewelers, had gone private only two and half years before it sold four million shares to the public. As another example, Dunlop Tire Corporation of Buffalo, New York, was resold to a Japanese company within five months of going private.

In these leveraged buyouts, pieces of the business are often sold off to retire the debt acquired in the buyout. This inevitably leaves a smaller company. Could personal loyalty come back because the businesses may be getting smaller and more focused, due to bursts of energy by high-powered, visionary entrepreneurs? Those who advance this argument usually bring up the idea of the hunting band. Here's an example from Norman Macrae, at the time the deputy editor of *The Economist:*

> Some modern and much criticized sociobiologists believe that man is an animal who has a genetic urge to hunt in packs, but also to make those packs less than 100 strong. . . .
>
> Big business corporations now face the difficulty that they are too large to inspire people to hunt together as a pack, so, behind many of their facades, the employees from just below the managing director to those around

the shop steward are forming separate packs to hunt each other....

The top 40 or so executives in a really big corporation do hunt together as a pack for the good of the dear old firm, even when stock options etc. do not tie their personal fortunes to its prosperity....

... However, there is for them an awkwardness of objective. The healthy driving force behind most efficient great international companies is competition (or, better, rivalry) against certain other great international companies in wanting to grow faster. But then, awkwardly, when they do grow, there is often a decline in their efficiency.

Often the new owners bring in new management, and this could imply new, personal loyalty, especially of the hunting band variety. For example, when the economy motel chain, Motel 6, went private, the new owners brought in new management. "Here was a situation where a company had unusual growth prospects and its main deficiency was its prior management," said the CEO of the bought-out version of the company.

The Two-Tier Setup

After the middle managers get bumped, upper management may suddenly discover that their former employees did useful work, which needs to get done. The solution? Get them back on a work-for-hire basis. The companies pay them less than before, offer no benefits, and get rid of them the day the job is done. This is the two-tier set-up. The top tier is composed of full-timers at the company, more or less enjoying the same sort of benefits as in the fat old days of corporate bloat. The second tier is the contractors, or vendors, as they're often called, trying to scratch out a day's income. Needless to say, there's little or no loyalty from either direction in this new two-tier set-up. But there is growth in the number of contractors. In 1986, according to management consultants A.T. Kearney, Inc., the percentage of total revenue spent on executives, managers, and supervisors declined by 2 percent. The percentage of revenue dumped in administrative expenses fell by nearly 5 percent. But the percentage of revenue handed over to contractors increased by almost 4 percent. Many believe this is the way nearly every company will be set up in the near future.

Can You Fake Loyalty?

"For those who've been fired during takeovers, the experience is like that of people with a traumatic memory of the Depression," says outplacement consultant Jay Bushell, who has counseled many of them. These people may be incapable of ever trusting an employer again, just as people who suffered through the Depression are often incapable of casually throwing money around. For them to fake loyalty would be the same as for those who starved during the Depression to walk into a crowded bar and shout "the drinks are on me!"

So what do you do? "You must develop behavior, not belief," counsels Bushell, adding, "always have a little voice saying 'how does this pay off for me?'" Beyond this, according to many job counselors, you must exhibit the obvious behaviors desired by employers that might substitute for loyalty: show up early, stay late, and, most important, show no signs of dissatisfaction, even if they're warranted.

Faking loyalty isn't an easy task, according to John Gallagher, now a professor at the Graduate School of Business, University of Chicago, but formerly the CEO of Chemetron, a Fortune 500 company. He says of phony loyalty, "If you try to look like it and you're not, it shows." According to Gallagher loyalty has been replaced with fit. "In talking to any executive for a principal position, you are looking to get a sense of whether the guy will fit into our culture. Most companies can abide a few characters, but not many," he says.

Suppose after the takeover you don't like the way things are being done in your department, a very common problem, as we've seen in several chapters in this book. You wisely decide not to cause problems by complaining about the boss. For all you know, he or she is doing exactly what top management wants. Recall the Heidrick and Struggles study on corporate loyalty. It looked at percentages of top managers subscribing to various definitions of loyalty. One definition—being a team player—was held by over 5 percent of top management. Add to this the over 6 percent who viewed loyalty as voicing an opinion but supporting the final decision. Then throw in another 33 percent who viewed loyalty as supporting corporate goals, strategies, philosophies, and policies. What do you get? Nearly a 50 percent chance that you'll be viewed as disloyal if you insist on doing things differently when all about you support the way things are being done.

If the company is big enough you could try to find a place in it where a person with your desire to make things better can succeed.

You could put in for a transfer. A well-connected manager would know exactly how to do this and whom to talk to on the quiet to avoid embarrassment. But junior people, or those who don't socialize sufficiently within the company, might go to personnel to see what's available or to discuss problems they're having in their current positions.

This should be a good idea, and a lot of companies post new openings for precisely this purpose. But there are questionable practices in this area that you should be alert to.

A major New York money center bank that had gone through a restructuring set up a sort of ombudsperson office in the human resources department to help resolve employee complaints. Naturally, employees were especially worried about possible retaliation, so they were assured by the company that any visits to the office would be discreet and confidential. There was clear evidence that this might be the case because appointments were scheduled so no one else would be around.

A counselor was waiting to hear the complaint *verbally*; nothing was written down. The idea was that the counselor would then try to straighten out the problem whatever way was possible. And the counselor always did, by taking notes after the complainer had left and showing them to the complainer's boss. The counselor and the boss then figured out together how to get rid of the squawking employee.

This should not surprise us. Columbia University professor Alan Westin, who is not the source of the story just recounted but is an expert on alternative dispute resolution procedures, has said in an interview that these procedures are almost never for managers. "It would be a career killer" to use them, says Westin. Managers are supposed to use the political process of the company to resolve problems. Those who can't do this don't fit in. Since this way of doing things is defined by many as part of the corporation's philosophies and policies, not to use the political process is to be disloyal. Essentially, for managers, these procedures are another test to determine who the disloyal people are in order to eliminate them.

Hence, we have the ultimate contradiction that makes this loyalty ordeal so difficult to address and overcome. Takeovers and other forces mentioned throughout this chapter would seem to make loyalty a moot point. Yet, at the same time, failure to live up to what the new top brass interpret as loyalty could be used as an excuse to boot you out the door. What's an ambitious manager to do under the circumstances? Going with the idea that loyalty is dead, outplacement counselor John Artise advises his clients to dispense with any assumptions of loyalty when they move to their next company. He counsels them to start negotiating before they get hired, clarifying the trade-offs, or, in his words, "what I get out of it, what you get out of it." He adds that not only are you likely to be taken advantage of if you don't do this, but "the employer will lose respect for you" if you don't look out for yourself from the start. University of Chicago professor Paul Hirsch calls this sort of negotiation being a "free agent manager," the term obviously borrowed from sports. Your task in the age of the takeover, then, is to walk the thin line of me-first free agency while putting in your hours and being aware of actions that could mark you as "disloyal" to the powers that be.

KEY POINTS

- Loyal managers who aren't high enough in the hierarchy to be rewarded for it with golden parachutes may be given "tin parachutes"—double the amount of severance pay they could expect to receive. However, the catch here is that a tin parachute is usually awarded only if the takeover is *hostile*.

- In addition to the increase in takeovers and restructurings, forces conspiring to break down loyalty are headhunters, computers and other forms of technology that replace people, and the influx of MBAs.

- Managers now average 8.8 years at one company as compared to 12 years of tenure, which was the norm as recently as 1981.

- This new reality of shorter terms of service at any one company has spawned new definitions of loyalty. For instance, there is "short-term loyalty"—where managers put forth their best effort at a company while having their resumé in constant circulation. And there is "personal loyalty"—loyalty to a specific individual or entrepreneur rather than to the firm itself.

- Don't ever try to *fake* loyalty. Try to find a place where you fit and cut the best deal going that you can.

10

THE TENTH ORDEAL
The Door

When a major automobile parts manufacturer was bought by a huge metals company, one of the most widely recognized people in the acquired company was the tax director, who had saved it huge bundles in the past few years. Confident that he, above all, would be retained, he was called in by the treasurer. "He said to me, 'I'm reorganizing the department; you're not part of it. I'd like you to pack your personal things and get out. Go talk to personnel about your rights,'" reported the tax director. "There was no handwriting on the wall," he said, adding, "After they fired me, I heard they sold the wall."

Sometimes, despite your best efforts to hang on, survival at your old company just isn't going to happen. This puts you in the final ordeal—being out on the street without the comparative comforts and occasional securities of the corporate set-up. What then? Three options people sometimes consider are to sue, search for another job, or become a consultant.

Suing

"I'm considering suing them," said the 55-year-old fired tax director for the auto parts manufacturing company. "The guy who replaced me was in his early thirties." Should he sue? Maybe, but maybe not.

On the plus side, says Wayne N. Outten, prominent New York plaintiff attorney, is that "he gets to stand up for his rights, and because of his age, he could get a jury trial under the Age Discrimination in Employment Act. But even with a jury, it's still not an automatic lock on a huge pile of cash." Outten adds that the downside also has to be looked at. "It's expensive, it can take a long time—from two to four years—and litigation is an awful drain, emotionally, physically, and financially." Outten knows what he's talking about. He's the co-author of the American Civil Liberties Union Handbook, *The Rights of Employees,* and head of the New York chapter of the Plaintiff Employment Lawyers Association, a nationwide group of about 500 solo practitioners and small firms that represent individuals who take on their former corporations.

Even if you win in these cases, the payoff may not be huge. In one case, Meg, a 60-year-old woman with 25 years of service to a Fortune 500 company, had worked her way up to lower management at a salary of $35,500 per year plus good benefits. Then a raider hit her company, and although it fought him off, it had to restructure as a result. Meg's position was eliminated. She had been at the middle level in a three-level department. The top person transferred to another city, so Meg applied for the top job. But it went to a 38-year-old woman with no experience. Meg was offered the bottom job with no cut in pay.

She resigned instead, taking early retirement, which was seven months of severance plus her pension. That's when she came to see Outten. They filed with the State Division of Human Rights. Outten reported what happened:

> At a conference before the hearing I told the company that our bottom line was $50,000. They offered $25,000, but I said $50,000 by the end of the week or we sue. The lawyer on the other side believed us—and he should have because we meant it. He phoned the company then and there and came back and agreed. They sent me the check. I kept my part and sent her hers.

By muscling the company, Meg got an additional year's severance.

Although obviously better off by threatening suit, the results did not resolve all Meg's financial worries. She searched for six months for another job and finally got one, with an hour's commute in each direction, making $18,500 a year as a legal secretary.

Outten and other plaintiff lawyers often caution against suing or even threatening to do so. For example, Paul H. Tobias, 57, a Cincinnati attorney who founded the Plaintiff Employment Lawyers Association, advised extreme caution to one of his clients. This irate 41-year-old man was the former head of personnel at a Fortune 500 company who lost his job after a takeover. The takeover started out unfriendly, but ended with top management smiling—except for the personnel director. He was immediately fired from his $150,000-a-year job despite some vague verbal promises from the old management that this wouldn't happen. He wasn't put out on the street empty-handed, however. The company gave him a severance package equivalent to a year-and-a-half's salary. But this didn't satisfy him. So he went to Tobias to see whether he had a wrongful discharge case, based on the idea that he placed *detrimental reliance*, to use legal lingo, on verbal promises that had been made to him. Even in states, such as New York, that give companies a nearly absolute right to fire under the legal doctrine of employment at will, you can sometimes snare the company on its own phony promises. "He was bitter, but I told him he was fortunate. He only had three year's service; he'd look silly to a jury, greedy. He took my advice and stopped complaining," says Tobias.

Not only does Tobias sometimes counsel against suing, he sometimes even advises his clients against letting the company know they've talked to a lawyer. The usual deal is that a manager gets sacked and is offered a severance package. "Three months is a frequent figure. The guy feels he should get a year, and I tell him he's right," says Tobias. But he doesn't tell him to sue or threaten to do so. Here's his advice:

> I always try to get them to negotiate it themselves, to avoid putting the company in a fighting mood. The guy should always be very discreet, maybe not even mention he's been to a lawyer. If they do want to drop in the word "lawyer," they could say "My wife says I should review this with a lawyer, but I don't want to. I have a lawyer but I've told him to go to hell, I don't want to give him a third."
>
> The goal is to make the company do the right thing. I tell them to go to their allies. But in a takeover, sometimes your allies aren't there anymore. They don't negotiate the golden parachutes the way they should. They take care of themselves. So you end up dealing with these new people who don't care. If the negotiations break down, then I step in and do the negotiating.

How successful are these negotiations? Says Tobias, who is in touch with the 500 members of his association:

> In the middle and lower management ranks, the companies are drawing the line. Negotiations are not typically successful in achieving excellent results where there are claims of age discrimination and the company has given three to six months of severance plus outplacement. If the company feels it's been generous and that you can't prove age discrimination and there are no smoking guns, you have to go to court, go through a year of discovery, then with the company facing a jury, they may settle. If we get past summary judgment, so the judge doesn't throw the case out, then we have maybe a 60 percent chance of winning, assuming the company has no misconduct case against the guy. But you have to have *some* evidence that age was a factor, such as if they replace the fired older guy with a younger person, or if there's a pattern that the older ones were laid off.

One thing lawyers can do for you is to help to package your arguments. People who are fired are in an emotional state and often don't know what their strongest arguments are. What are a few of these cases that they can make? For some managers, the strongest case is that they know where the bodies are buried. For others, the argument will be designed to elicit guilt on the part of those who have fired them. Still others will try to mobilize their friends to improve the severance package. Timing is important in this case, since it has to be done while both the person about to be fired and his friends are still on the team and also before a decision has been finalized. "Try to get in there before an official position has been taken," advises Tobias. Sometimes the strongest argument is equity. If you know that similarly situated people have been getting more than you have, you may be able to get more yourself. One executive who had been making $100,000 a year before he was bumped after a takeover was offered three months' severance. After talking with Tobias, he asked around and found out that others in his position were getting a year or more. "When he presented those facts to the company, they crumbled," says Tobias. Incidentally, in this case, the company never knew the executive had a lawyer.

Are you finished in the corporate world if you sue? "Once you're identified as a whistleblower or troublemaker, you're gone," says Tobias, adding, "For example, the victims of sexual harassment, no matter how justified their suits may be, are usually through."

Other plaintiff lawyers agree. "That may indeed be true," says Diane Serafin Blank, 41, a New York attorney well known for handling sexual harassment cases, who adds, "But I don't know if sexual harassment cases are different from any other type of suit against the company." Ms. Blank says she cannot think of a single case where a middle management woman has won a big bucks settlement for sexual harassment and then gone on to a successful corporate career. This could be a relevant issue in takeovers, since according to Ms. Blank and others, women appear to be fired in disproportionate numbers during the takeover, and some of these firings may mask sexual harassment.

So the conclusion on suing your company is: Only do it if you figure you've got nothing to lose.

Getting Another Job

Assuming you don't sue, and therefore aren't branded as trouble, what about getting another job? How do you start? Nearly everyone recommends outplacement if your company will pay for it. However, some plaintiff lawyers urge that you forget the outplacement and instead ask your company for the cash equivalent, which could be $10,000 or more. This advice may be based on the assumption that if you're talking to a lawyer and planning to sue, you're never going to get another corporate job anyway.

Many plaintiff lawyers, however, do recommend outplacement. For example, Paul Tobias says, "I think outplacement is good because of the camaraderie of the people—a lot of similarly situated people, from whom you get companionship, and a chance for the catharsis which comes from unloading your rage. It helps repair your damaged self-esteem."

You also get a place to go, so you don't sit around the house and fall apart from depression. The place, of course is basically an office for those without jobs, but it has a phone and desk at your disposal and someone to answer the phone in case a possible employer is trying to get hold of you. Nearly always there's help in resumé writing and advice on making contacts—networking. Some of the network is right there in the room: People trade contacts. If top management at your company is too mean-hearted or cheap to spring for outplacement, you might want to pay for it yourself. Kennedy & Kennedy, Inc. in Fitzwilliam, New Hampshire, publishes a *Directory of Outplacement Firms*. You could use it to see whether any in your area are to your liking. Don't neglect the advice of the Federal

Trade Commission, which suggests in a pamphlet that you "check with local consumer protection agencies to see if they have received any complaints about an employment company with whom you intend to sign a contract." These agencies can also tell you about state laws regulating these firms.

Then there's the executives' outplacement kibbutz, Forty Plus, with chapters in New York; Buffalo; Oakland, California; Los Angeles; Laguna Drive, California; Denver; Fort Collins; Colorado Springs; Columbus; Dallas; Honolulu; Houston; Philadelphia; Washington, D.C.; and Toronto. They're all listed in the phone books in those cities. Although some outplacement offices have been described by managers who've used them as "morgues," Forty Plus chapters tend to be anything but depressing. Walking into one is like walking into the frenzy of a political campaign office a week before the election. People there are busy hustling up new job possibilities, setting up meetings, doing detailed critiques of each other's resumés, holding mock job interviews. Don't go to a Forty Plus chapter if you want to be depressed, because you won't have time for it. A lot of people get jobs because of those places, perhaps mainly because they jack up their energy levels. They're also cheap. Typically the price comes to around five hundred dollars for the duration, and you usually have to put in a couple of days a week working at the office. Nearly everyone who does it says it's well worth it.

Two people who say so are John Ziebarth, 49, and Annette Carrar, 41. They were sitting across the table from each other at various meetings of the New York chapter of Forty Plus. Ziebarth joined after leaving a consumer products manufacturing business. Carrar had previously had her own brokerage business, which she sold. But this required that she sign a noncompete agreement. So she spent the next year and a half working for a retail clothing business. When the noncompete agreement was up and she could legitimately get back into her field, she decided she didn't want to be a broker anymore. So she joined Forty Plus as the best approach to getting back into the financial services industry.

Forty Plus has a lot of workshops, including one called the "Job Jury," in which members spend an hour or so in a constructive critique of another member's resumé. During these and other panels, Ziebarth reports that he and Carrar "discovered we had different but complementary skills and experiences, so we decided we would team up and apply for openings for management teams."

Teams? It's hard enough to get one job, let alone two. True, but, according to Ziebarth, the leading graduate schools of business send out alumni newsletters, which do from time to time list team openings. Sometimes these are blind listings and the prospective team has to go through the specific alumni office, but not always. So the trick is to get hold of the alumni newsletters. Once again, Forty Plus enters the picture. The New York chapter, and quite possibly many of the others, have members who are alumni from most of the good schools, and they bring in and circulate these newsletters.

Ziebarth and Carrar applied for several of these positions and eventually landed a modified one—they were both hired as a team for one job, in place of the chief financial officer of a start-up company, a storage service business for the military. However, for tax and legal reasons, the two of them formed a legal partnership.

Where are you most likely to get a job? At a new or small business. Here's what David L. Birch, an expert on small business, has to say about the deluge of new businesses:

> In 1985, almost 700,000 new companies were formed, compared with 90,000 start-ups in 1950 and only 200,000 even as recently as 1965. These 700,000 new businesses are in addition to approximately 400,000 new partnerships and 300,000 newly self-employed people. In short, about 1.4 million new enterprises of some sort were created last year.

Of course, most of these companies are very small. But at the same time that they were being created, Birch points out, about 1.4 million new jobs were also created, which works out to about one new job for each new enterprise. Also at the same time, the big companies were bumping people from their work forces. "The Fortune 500 companies alone employed 2.2 million fewer people at the end of 1985 than they did at the beginning of 1980," says Birch.

So this means that, setting all other factors aside, the most likely area to get a new job is in a smaller business; the odds are better there than in a Fortune 500 company. Many consultants make the same point. For example, James E. Barrett, 57, the managing director of Philadelphia's Cresheim Management Consulting, has said:

> The good news for middle management is that the guy over 50 who used to be unemployable now is employable again if he doesn't get in his own way. He has to be flexible on status and titles since the kind of company that will hire him doesn't want high fixed costs. So they should go for jobs at smaller companies and go for a relatively smaller salary and big bonuses.

However, this brings us back to one of the more unpleasant facts of takeovers. The middle manager who thought he might finally be able to have a better deal at the corporation now has the same sort of deal he had when starting out—working dreadful hours and not collecting commensurate pay.

When discussing the perfect resumé form, ten headhunters may give ten different pieces of advice, but there is consensus on one point: The fired manager should get his story straight. The Association of Executive Search Consultants, Inc. has published a pamphlet by the president of one of its member firms, William C. Houze and Company. It is entitled "Before the Resume—establish a rational foundation that will withstand the rigors of a job campaign." Bill Houze advises that job candidates develop a *rationale*—"a summary statement expressing to prospective employers the totality of your reason, or reasons, for seeking a new situation." In other words, how come you left your old job?

Houze says that this rationale must meet a five-pronged test. First, it must be true, meaning that when others are queried on it, they will say something like, "Yes, that is about the way things happened." Second, your rationale must be understandable. This means job interviewers can get it quickly and easily; it's not complex and convoluted. Third, the rationale must be believable. If it strains credibility, even if true, you'll have to figure out a way to package it so it's more believable. Fourth, the rationale has to be acceptable—to the industry, the company, and the interviewer. For example, if you were dumped during the takeover because you didn't meet a profit or sales goal, you should find a prospective employer who is not pathologically concerned about that sort of thing. Fifth, the rationale has to be comfortable. You have to feel at home with it or else you won't be able to pitch yourself properly.

Consulting

"Consulting has glamour," explains Irving Shaw, president of the Society of Professional Management Consultants, adding, "You're often with the president of the company. If you're a solo practitioner, you're your own boss, and you can get in with no investment except a business card."

Consulting can be a very appealing and lucrative activity. You can cash in on contacts at your old company, perhaps consulting for them. For many people, consulting is fun.

But it has problems too.

The Door

"The hardest part of consulting is to get a chance to sit across the table from the guy who might say no," says John F. Hartshorne, the Executive Director of the Institute of Management Consultants, the major organization that accredits individual consultants with the label CMC, Certified Management Consultant.

Getting the business is usually the toughest part of consulting. "If you've gotten as far as sitting across the table from a prospective client," says Hartshorne, "you've got somebody who must have some degree of interest in what you're talking about, so the probability is that you'll walk out with a chance to submit a proposal." Submit a proposal? What about a deal? A retainer agreement? A regular spot in the executive parking lot? Not so fast. Before the dotted line comes the pitched line in the form of a proposal, which itself may take several days of unpaid work, and was only obtained by spending an hour or two talking to the client about his problem, for which you may have had to drive for hours—perhaps from the local airport, having flown in to make the pitch. And all of this at your own expense.

"If you have that chance to submit a proposal," continues Hartshorne, "then you've got at least a 50/50 chance of getting a consulting job—on a project basis, which is the way nearly all consulting is done."

Take the case of Fredrica Levinson, a solo practitioner in human resource consulting for about a year at the time of this writing. Her firm, in Teaneck, New Jersey, is named FSL Human Resource Services. She's learned the hard way about the 50/50 chance, and the amazing frequency with which one of those 50 percents keeps coming up. "There are a lot of promises in this business that don't pan out," she cautions. She cites as a typical example the case of the director of training of a major manufacturing corporation. In this case, Levinson lucked through the hardest part. "She called me," reports Levinson, "and told me she'd established 14 training programs, each two hours long, paying $500 apiece. You can't wait until you get a contract; you have to submit an outline of the training module, in my case on communication skills."

This she did, putting in a good deal of preparation to tailor the two hours to the needs of this specific company. Her proposal was good, so the response was as well. Then, silence. Naturally, Levinson did what any effective business person does—followed up. "I spoke to her recently. She said corporate is reviewing her program. It's questionable that it will go."

This and similar experiences have made Ms. Levinson take a sober view of interested potential clients. She reports, for example,

"When a gentleman from an academic institution said, 'Boy, can we use you,' I can't tell you how many times I've heard that. My eyes used to light up." But now she may be squinting with suspicion. "Those potential clients are well meaning," she adds, "but they don't always have the power, and even when they do, its not a priority."

But it hasn't been all bad. "I was damn lucky when I started. I landed two very good clients who kept me intensely busy for four months. One project is still ongoing. But during those four months, I made a mistake. I didn't keep drumming up business. I woke up one day and said, 'I don't have any work.'"

"My most difficult decision was what to specialize in," says Elizabeth Quinn of QuinnEssentials, Inc., of Manhattan. Five years ago she had been the VP of distribution planning for Citibank. During her years there she had seen Citicorp acquire both Diners Club and Carte Blanche, and so had seen mergers from the dominant side. This gave her a sense of what was coming in the corporate world, and she decided to get out. "I was 38 years old, and I figured if I failed during the usual failure time period of two to five years, I'd still be young enough to go back in. Luckily, I didn't have to go back."

Although she had specialized knowledge in a wide range of planning areas, including marketing planning, site location, and capital planning for technology purchases, she decided to focus on microcomputers. Did she make that decision by applying her knowledge of planning? Sort of—after the market for it came to her. "A personal acquaintance, the president of an oriental rug business, asked if I could help automate their business," she reports, adding, "It was the most natural thing for me because it called upon all my general skills in evaluating a business and selecting solutions that would meet their needs. And the field was only one year old then. I now consult on the types of microcomputer systems to set up."

If this was the toughest decision, it wasn't the hardest part of setting up the business, which was *getting* the business. "When I started I had one client and lots of time," she reports, adding, "I could see money coming in two weeks ahead. By two years later, I made a profit. In the interim I borrowed from my parents—I went in without any capital or backing."

How did she get the business? She explains: "I got on the phone and called everyone I knew. My first calls were not successful because I said 'I'm a consultant and I can do everything,' which left all the thinking to them, a bad idea." Not until she focused on personal computer systems did her business start to go. "By the second year I developed a major corporate client," she recalls, "and then I started a second business, software for ad agencies and public relations firms. It does time and purchase accounting against jobs, helping with billing and profit analysis. Now even the consultant business has turned into a software development company."

Getting the business was only one of the difficulties. "The other hard part was cabin fever," reports Quinn, adding, "It was extremely difficult to be alone. The corporate world is ideal for a gregarious person, so much time is spent managing people on a one-on-one basis or in meetings—you spend very little time alone."

This comment is typical. For this reason, James H. Kennedy, a well known and widely respected authority on consulting, says "Absolutely, join a professional consulting organization. Consulting is a very lonely business and you can't confide in clients, it's embarrassing." Kennedy has his preeminent position in the field because he is the publisher of a number of widely read works in the area, including the major newsletter, *Consultants News*, and the *Directory of Management Consultants*, published in Fitzwilliam, New Hampshire. Kennedy also has his own consulting practice, devoted exclusively to consulting to other consultants.

Kennedy and quite a few others have also pointed out the value of the Fundamentals of Consulting seminars offered by associations such as John Hartshorne's New-York-based IMC or the association composed largely of solo practitioners, the Society of Professional Management Consultants, headquartered in Englewood, New Jersey. These seminars give pointers on the human relations part of consulting, which, according to Hartshorne, is "critical to the success of the relationship. If the client doubts your sincerity, integrity, competence, or just plain doesn't like you, they won't accept your recommendations. You'll have a failed project and your reputation will catch up with you."

Hartshorne, Kennedy, and others also advise that attending annual meetings of the various associations allows you to pick up additional pointers and gets you in touch with other consultants, who can be quite helpful. "These are sharing experiences, with people coming from all over the country," says Kennedy.

"Knowing other independent consultants leads to business," adds Irving Shaw, president of the association of one-person firms. Shaw has his own one-man consulting practice in Wayne, New Jersey. One way his association might get you business is through networking, and a second way is through the referral program the organization maintains.

Shaw points out another advantage to joining an organization such as his own. "For people starting out, it helps with image, like having a good business card, a good address, a good phone exchange, and good report covers—anything which establishes professionalism." Shaw, however, does not necessarily recommend starting one's own solo practice. "I'd recommend that middle managers start in an existing firm; it's easier than starting one's own business," he says.

If you think this is a good idea, where do you start looking? You could begin by getting Kennedy's *Directory* and contacting the firms in it, and you might also subscribe to his newsletter, to get in touch with the gossip and comings and goings of the industry. There is no Big Eight of the consulting world, although all of the Big Eight accounting firms do have consulting subunits. But there *is* something like the Fortune 500 of consulting.

These are the 60 member firms of ACME, founded a few months before the stockmarket crash in 1929 by former associates of the time and motion man, Frederick Taylor. ACME, which used to be called the Association of Consulting Management Engineers but today simply uses the acronym, is where many of the larger management consulting firms belong. According to its president, Joseph J. Brady, of the 65,000 management consultants in the United States, some 28,000 are with the 60 ACME firms. In 1987, about $3.5 billion will be billed worldwide by these ACME member firms. Of this, using 1986 data, the last year for which data were available, about $1.5 billion was billed by the consulting subunits of Big Eight accounting firms—members of ACME all. This represented a steady increase over previous years. How much of this is generated in the United States? No figures are available, but the total billings in this industry in the United States in 1987 has been estimated at about $5 billion. Obviously, the 60 ACME firms account for a huge chunk of this. Add to them Booze-Allen & Hamilton, and McKinsey & Company, two giants in the industry, and the picture becomes clear that 62 firms probably account for the lion's share of the billings, and the other thousands of consultants scramble for what's left.

Furthermore, according to a 1987 speech by Dr. Marvin Schiller, ACME's chairman, the biggest firms are getting bigger, and the medium-sized ones, with average billings of at least $5 million per year, are staying about the same size. The bigger ones are getting bigger, incidentally, in many cases through the process which prompted this book—takeovers. For example, Towers, Perrin, Forster, and Crosby, which specializes in actuarial/benefits has bought Cresap, McCormick, and Paget, as well as Case and Company Tillinghast, Nelson & Warren, Telesis and also Hayes/Hill.

The consulting business has grown steadily over the years, with the exception of a dip during the 1982 recession, and continues to grow at about 14 to 18 percent per year in billings, according to ACME. Why the growth? "Consultants prosper in times of change," says Brady. Here are the changes he ticked off in an interview: globalization of markets; a massive explosion of information; new, computer-driven manufacturing techniques; the transferring of management functions outside of the organization—buying instead of making. All of these trends are obviously going to continue at least for the next few years, so consulting should continue to grow.

How much do the Big Boys make? Not as much as you might think. According to both Brady and Edward D. Hendricks, the vice president of ACME, a senior partner at a major firm is making a base salary of about $120,000 a year. They also divide up whatever the firm's net is at the end of the year. Keep in mind, also, that their whole lives may be run through the partnership, which could own their cars, houses, and so forth. Even so, according to Brady, very few consultants are making as much as $325,000 a year altogether. "I know just one who is," says Brady. So any number of Yuppee corporate liquidators on Wall Street are making much more.

Moving back to Planet Earth, how much could you get on your first job? Jim Kennedy advises billing out at between $500 and $750 per day as a start-up, solo consultant. How much could you make as a solo? Irving Shaw thinks that the typical income of a member of his group is about $50,000, "but that's strictly a guess," he cautions. Jim Kennedy, however, may have more accurate data. "Nobody ever lies to me because they know I'd cream 'em in the newsletter if I ever found out," he says. He has recently written about two solos who are raking in the cash. One in Milwaukee clears over $100,000 a year by consulting to small businesses, and another in New York City clears over $250,000 by specializing in purchasing management for large corporations.

Some consultants advise companies on what to do after a takeover and resulting restructuring have left their buildings empty and their land seemingly useless. "Companies cannot legally raise the book value of their depreciated properties because then they would be taking a depreciation twice," says Richard Nymark, president of Nycor Associates, Inc., of New York City. He advises large corporations on how to turn fully depreciated plants and surplus property, the mere smell of which may cause corporate raiders to drool all over their thousand-dollar suits, into productive assets. "There are legal and ethical ways to do it," he says, and he has advised a number of Fortune 1000 companies on what they are.

Consultants can even prosper during hard times. For example, Bert Behrendt, 57, is a solo practitioner located in Lake Oswego, a suburb of Portland. The area has not fully recovered from the last recession, but he does very well consulting to hotels and resorts. Eight years ago he got fed up with being moved every two years as general manager of one Sheraton hotel after another, so he decided to stay put in Portland because he likes the Pacific Northwest.

Even with this background, he had two tough years getting established as a consultant. "It takes time to establish a track record," says Behrendt, adding, "People say 'How do I know you're good at what you say you're good at?'" Evidently the word got out, since he's now making more money than he was as a general manager. He's also on retainer to two five-star hotels, the highest designation in this country, and is referred by banks to help turn around other hotels that they have taken possession of.

His advice: "Specialize in a certain area and be better than anyone else. Mediocrity doesn't sell." Behrendt specializes in two areas within hotel management—food and beverages, and sales and controls. "Anybody who says he's an expert in every area of hotel management is full of hot air," says Behrendt. And that's a former general manager at several major hotels speaking.

He also strongly urges that consultants be absolutely honest. "The only thing I have to sell is competence, honesty, and sincerity," he says, concluding, "If I compromised those values I'd have no right to be in business and I don't think I would be in business."

"Those who can, do. Those who can't, teach," said George Bernard Shaw in one of his most frequently quoted lines. But consultants are rapidly raising doubts about this quip, since a lot of them are both advisers and doers.

David D. Humphrey, of Holland, Ohio, is an example. He advises trucking companies on the paperwork involved in interstate trucking, but also handles the whole paperwork operation for them. According to Humphrey:

> Every time a truck enters a new state it's like entering a separate country; the state public service commission regulates trucking, the state department of revenue goes after the taxes, and the state's secretary of state issues the license plates. The issue is so complicated and changes so fast that most attorneys don't want to bother with it— they come to me, and I'm not an attorney.

He's now performed these services for over 250 trucking companies, some of them fairly large, with fleets of trucks. But things weren't always so good. "I had four or five clients when I started, and the first year was very hard. I had to do a lot of knocking on doors. Now everything comes from current client referrals," he reports.

The story of how this company began is worth noting. "I started this as a whole division of another small company, but the owner and I didn't see eye to eye, so I took my clients with me and left," recalls Humphrey.

Nearly every successful consultant works killer hours. According to Jim Kennedy, those making $50,000 or more typically have 200 days a year of billings and put in 80- to 90-hour weeks.

Typical of the killer pace is that worked by Lin Kroeger, 35, who set up her own one-woman consulting business, The Communication Link Company, Inc., in Florham Park, New Jersey. She realized that technical people, such as auditors and systems personnel, sometimes have, as she puts it, "the hardest time making communications work for them." But to make their shortcomings in communications work for her, Lin has had to work staggering hours from the very beginning. "For the first two years, they were close to 80 hours per week, not including travel time—every minute of my life was devoted to this business." However, the last three years have eased up. "I no longer work weekends unless I'm in a dire emergency. I'm usually here between 7:30 and 8:00 A.M. and leave between 8:00 and 10:00 P.M.," she reports.

So the easy times are a mere 60 to 70 hours per week. Consultants don't succeed unless they have a light touch with people. But since they have to labor like hell, this is a profession for ladies and gentlemen who work like maniacs.

However, there's one big advantage to working all these hours. You're not on the street, unless you're rushing to another consulting job. And you're way too busy to be upset about the takeover and its ordeals, which you've left behind in the dust.

KEY POINTS

- You may be able to sue for age or sex discrimination, but win or lose you will probably be branded as a troublemaker in the corporate world. If you get enough money, don't want to go back, or can't go back, this may not matter.

- Consulting a lawyer may be a good idea even if you don't intend to sue, since he could help you frame your arguments for a better severance deal, and, if you can't make a better deal, maybe he can do it for you, even without threatening a suit.

- You can find a lawyer through the Plaintiff Employment Lawyer's Association, which has chapters in all states and might be listed in the phone book in your city. If not, contact its founder, Paul Tobias, in Cincinnati.

- Nearly everyone recommends outplacement as a good idea. A kibbutz version of it is Forty Plus.

- The best place to look for another job may be in smaller companies, but be flexible in your demands.

- Although there is no consensus on the ideal resumé form, there is agreement that you should get your story straight before you talk to any prospective employers.

- Although consulting can be glamorous and lucrative, it is also a very tough grind at first. The hardest part is getting the business.

- A good idea when you start out is to join a consulting association and take a course in how to consult offered by such associations as the Institute of Management Consultants. A subscription to *Consulting News* would also be wise, since it lets you know who's doing what in the profession.

NOTES

Introduction

Page

2   State power over takeovers: Stuart Taylor Jr., "High Court Backs State on Curbing Hostile Takeover," *The New York Times*, April 22, 1987.

2   Congressman Dingell's bill: Bruce Ingersoll, "Dingell, Markey Seek to Curb Raids via Open Market," *The Wall Street Journal*, April 27, 1987.

2   Reagan Administration opposition to the Congressional bills on takeovers: William Kronholm, "White House Hits Bill to Curb Raiders," *The Washington Post*, June 24, 1987.

2   Role of tax changes in the stock market crash: Robert J. Cole, "Takeover Stocks Up Sharply," *The New York Times*, October 30, 1987.

2   Statistics on takeovers for 1984 through 1986: Very kindly supplied by Alex Ladias of W.T. Grimm & Co., Chicago. Figures for

---

All quotations in the text not referenced here are taken from interviews by the author.

the first five months of 1987: Brian Burrough, "Reports of Takeover Demise Are Greatly Exaggerated," *The Wall Street Journal*, June 26, 1987.

3   Firing of Continental Group's corporate staff: Reported to the author in interviews with several of those involved.

3   Lamalie survey, Hayes/Hill survey, and figures for Crocker National Bank: Susan R. Sanderson and Lawrence Schein, "Sizing Up the Down-Sizing Era," *Across the Board*, November 1986.

4   Government statistic showing 75% of managers bouncing back from job displacement: U.S. Congress, Office of Technology Assessment, *Technology and Structural Unemployment—Reemploying Displaced Adults* (Washington, D.C.: U.S. Government Printing Office, February 1986), p. 110.

4   BLS statistics on the change in pay: Ibid., p. 116.

4   Bureau of International Labor Affairs survey: Ibid., p. 115.

4   Twenty-seven weeks with no job: Ibid, p. 110.

4   *Fortune* survey: "Pushed Out at 45—Now What?" *Fortune*, March 2, 1987, p. 29.

5   Professor Jenson: *Corporate Takeovers—Part 1*, Hearings before the Subcommittee on Telecommunications, Consumer Protection, and Finance of the Committee on Energy and Commerce, House of Representatives, Ninety-Ninth Congress, First Session, February 27, March 12, April 23, and May 22, 1985, Serial No. 99-99, p. 228.

5   Joseph Wright: Ibid., p. 169.

5   Henry G. Manne: F.M. Scherer, "Takeovers: Present and Future Dangers," *The Brookings Review*, Winter/Spring 1986.

6   T. Boone Pickens: *Corporate Takeovers—Part 1*, Hearings before the Subcommittee on Telecommunications, Consumer Protection, and Finance of the Committee on Energy and Commerce, House of Representatives, Ninety-Ninth Congress, First Session, February 27, March 12, April 23, and May 22, 1985, Serial No. 99-99, p. 74.

6 Leigh Trevor: "Hostile Takeovers—The Killing Field of Corporate America," given to the Financial Executives Institute (Northeast Ohio Chapter), March 11, 1986, and published by Jones, Day, Reavis & Pogue, Cleveland, Ohio.

7 Anecdotes and quotes on successful restructuring: Myron Magnet, "Restructuring Really Works," *Fortune*, March 2, 1987.

7 Facts on Phillips: Interview with Phillips' CEO, Pete Silas, and from "Hostile Takeovers—The Killing Field of Corporate America," address by Leigh B. Trevor of Jones, Day, Reavis & Pogue to the Financial Executives Institute (Northeast Ohio Chapter), March 11, 1986.

7 *Business Week's* cover story: "Do Mergers Really Work?" June 3, 1985.

8 Arguments for and against stock market price significance in mergers and the study of profits: F.M. Scherer, "Takeovers: Present and Future Dangers," *The Brookings Review*, Winter/Spring 1986.

9 List of objections to hostile takeovers: "Hostile Takeovers—The Killing Field of Corporate America," address by Leigh B. Trevor of Jones, Day, Reavis & Pogue to the Financial Executives Institute (Northeast Ohio Chapter), March 11, 1986.

9 Figure on 1984's equity flight: Andrew Sigler in *Corporate Takeovers—Part 2*, Hearings before the Subcommittee on Telecommunications, Consumer Protection, and Finance of the Committee on Energy and Commerce, House of Representatives, Ninety-Ninth Congress, First Session, May 23, June 12, and October 24, 1985, p. 196.

9 Quote on R&D: Walter Adams and James W. Brock, "The Hidden Costs of Failed Mergers," *The New York Times*, June 21, 1987.

9 David Weber: "Fee-ding Frenzy," *California Business*, April 1987.

9 Corky and Orky: Tim Waters, "Publisher Fights Image of Bad Guy," *Los Angeles Times*, April 26, 1987.

The First Ordeal—The Niagara of Rumors

13 C.J. "Pete" Silas: Telephone interview. Other Phillips data: Interview with George Meese, Phillips' Corporate Secretary.

13   Robert J. Lee: Robert Bell, "You *Can* Survive a Company Takeover," *Dynamic Years*, November–December 1985.

13   Andrew Sigler: Steven E. Prokesch, "'People Trauma' in Mergers," *The New York Times*, November 19, 1985.

14   Data on AMF, Conwed, and McQuay, Inc.: "Stakeholders In America, Research Committee, Background Information." Some details on Conwed are from Mike Langberg, "Conwed Workers Construct New Lives After Takeover," The *St. Paul Pioneer Press and Dispatch*, November 3, 1986.

14   Leigh Trevor: "Hostile Takeovers—The Killing Field of Corporate America," address by Leigh Trevor of Jones, Day, Reavis & Pogue to the Financial Executives Institute (Northeast Ohio Chapter), March 11, 1986.

15   Kathleen Kucera: "Mergers and Acquisitions: Investor Relations Victims Speak Out," *The Corporate Communications Report*, Volume 16, Number 4, October 1985.

16   Silicon Valley: Christopher H. Schmitt, "Why the Industry's Glory Days May Be Over," *San Jose Mercury News*, December 1, 1986.

17   Price Pritchett: Price Pritchett, *After the Merger: Managing the Shock Waves* (Homewood, IL: Dow Jones Irwin, 1985), p. 46.

17   Various types of job recruiting techniques, including the grapevine: Wendell L. French, *Human Resources Management* (Boston: Houghton Mifflin Company, 1986), pp. 242–243.

17   Layoffs at AMD: Christopher H. Schmitt, "Why the Industry's Glory Days May Be Over," *San Jose Mercury News*, December 1, 1986.

18   GAO study on notice time: Mary A.C. Fallon and Ray Alvareztorres, "Out of Work—Overnight," *San Jose Mercury News*, June 16, 1986.

18   Boesky case grapevine: "A Chronology of the Wall Street Scandal," *The Wall Street Journal*, February 13, 1987.

18   Boesky's quote: Ivan Boesky, *Merger Mania* (New York: Holt, Rinehart and Winston, 1985), p. 14.

18 SEC study on the jump in stock prices before merger announcements: "Stocks Rise Sharply Before Tender Bids, SEC Study Finds," *The New York Times*, March 11, 1987.

19 Stephen A. Schwarzman: Stephen A. Schwarzman, "Cures for the Insider Problems; First Set Higher Ethical Standards . . ." *The New York Times*, March 8, 1987. Copyright © 1987 by The New York Times Company. Reprinted by permission.

21 Burlington/Edelman story: Alison Leigh Cowan, "Insider Cited in Burlington Bid," *The New York Times*, June 10, 1987. Copyright © 1987 by The New York Times Company. Reprinted by permission.

21 Ernest Sando: "Mergers and Acquisitions: Investor Relations Victims Speak Out," *The Corporate Communications Report*, Volume 16, Number 4, October 1985.

22 Background data on CBS: "Stakeholders in America, Research Committee, Background Information."

23 Boyer article: Peter J. Boyer, "Sadness Turns to Anger Over CBS Dismissals," *The New York Times*, March 9, 1987. Andy Rooney and Mike Wallace: same article. Copyright © 1987 by The New York Times Company. Reprinted by permission.

23 Details of the CBS News restructuring and the quotes of Dan Rather and Tisch's reply to Rather: Peter J. Boyer, "CBS News Chief Gives Plan For Cuts," *The New York Times*, March 5, 1987. Copyright © 1987 by The New York Times Company. Reprinted by permission.

24 Quote from IBM: Robert Levering, Milton Moskowitz, and Michael Katz, *The 100 Best Companies to Work For in America* (New York: New American Library, 1985), p. 164.

24 IBM/Rolm story: David E. Sanger, "IBM Enfolds Much of Rolm," *The New York Times*, March 12, 1987. Copyright © 1987 by The New York Times Company. Reprinted by permission.

25 Price Pritchett: Price Pritchett, *After the Merger: Managing the Shock Waves* (Homewood, IL: Dow Jones Irwin, 1985), p. 47.

25 Figure of 95% accuracy of information carried by the grapevine: Arthur G. Bedeian, *Management* (New York: The Dryden Press, 1986), p. 534.

26 Pete Silas: Quoted from telephone interview.

28 MacDonald, and Miller: Alison Leigh Cowan, "Tisch is Holding a Hot Potato," *The New York Times*, March 14, 1987. Copyright © 1987 by The New York Times Company. Reprinted by permission.

The Second Ordeal—Who Are These Guys?

38 Robert Montgomery: Quoted from interviews and from "New York Human Resource Advisory Council Tackles Reference Checking," in *News Report*, published by the Association of Executive Search Consultants, Inc., Fall 1985.

39 Wanda L. Ellert: Quoted from interview and her article, "Reference Checking: The Legal Perspective," in *News Report*, published by the Association of Executive Search Consultants, Inc., Fall 1985.

42 Jemison and Sitkin: David Jemison and Sim Sitkin, "Acquisitions: The Process Can Be a Problem," *Harvard Business Review*, March–April 1986.

45 Howard Raiffa: Howard Raiffa, *The Art and Science of Negotiation*, The Belknap Press of Harvard University Press, 1982, p. 182.

The Third Ordeal—The Anglo Saxons Versus the Normans

50 "The way we do things around here": quoted from Terrence E. Deal and Allen A. Kennedy, *Corporate Cultures—The Rites and Rituals of Corporate Life* (Reading, MA: Addison-Wesley Publishing Company, 1982), p. 4.

50 *Psychology Today:* Mitchell Lee Marks and Philip Harold Mirvis, "The Merger Syndrome," October 1986. Reprinted with permission from Psychology Today Magazine copyright © 1986.

52 Fast-track pay survey: "News From AESC," press release, Association of Executive Search Consultants, February 26, 1987.

52 Accountants' merger: Lee Burton, "Mixed Marriages," *The Wall Street Journal*, April 22, 1987.

53 Korn/Ferry survey: Korn Ferry International's Executive Profile: "A Survey of Corporate Leaders in the Eighties," New York, 1986.

55 Philip H. Mirvis, "Negotiations After the Sale: The Roots and Ramifications of Conflict in an Acquisition." *Journal of Occupational Behavior*, Vol 6, 65–84 (1985).

55 McKinsey Staff Paper on corporate cultures: "How Corporate Parents Add Value," by Stephen C. Coley, John Patience, and Sigurd Reinton, May 1986, No. 30.

57 McKinsey Staff Paper on the failure rates on acquisitions: Steve Coley, "Diversification Through Acquisition," McKinsey White Paper, undated.

58 Ethnic, sex, and religious data: Korn/Ferry International's Executive Profile: "A Survey of Corporate Leaders in the Eighties," New York, 1986, p. 23.

60 "Powerlessness and helplessness": Philip H. Mirvis, "Negotiations After the Sale: The Roots and Ramifications of Conflict in an Acquisition," *Journal of Occupational Behavior*, Vol. 6, 65–84 (1985).

60 Mary Kennan: Gayle Feldman, "Anatomy of an Acquisition," *Publishers Weekly*, July 3, 1987.

64 McKinsey White Paper: Steve Coley, "Diversification Through Acquisition," undated.

65 Phillip Morris: Ibid, p. 2

65 Xerox: Ibid., p. 3

65 "Analysis of 18 recent acquisitions": Ibid, p. 3

65 "Seller initiated": Ibid. p. 6

65 "Reactive responses": Ibid. p. 6

65 "Value adding levers": Ibid. p. 3

66 "Stripping over-funded pension plans": Ibid., p. 4

66 "Successful acquirers appear to": "Empirical Success of Acquisition Programs McKinsey & Company, Inc.," undated McKinsey White Paper.

The Fourth Ordeal—Nothing Is Getting Done

70   GM: Amal Kumar Naj, "GM Now Is Plagued With Drop in Morale as Payrolls Are Cut," *Wall Street Journal*, May 26, 1987.

74   Woo Woo: Robert Bell, "Est Gets Dressed For Success," *Venture*, March 1987.

75   Werner Erhard: Ibid.

75   Tom Peters: Mark Bowie, "The Transformation Game," *Image*, October 12, 1986. The quote has been independently confirmed by the author of this book with Tom Peters.

76   Price Pritchett: Price Pritchett, *Making Mergers Work*, (Homewood, IL: Dow Jones Irwin, 1987), Chapters 3 and 5.

The Fifth Ordeal—The Scramble To Fit In

86   Davidson: Jeffrey P. Davidson, *Blow Your Own Horn*, (New York: AMACOM, 1987), Chapter 6.

95   Relocation factors: Paul Hobson-Panico, "Relocation Profile Pre-Move Assessment, Summary Technical Report" (Boulder, CO: Moran, Stahl & Boyer, Inc.)

96   Michael Tucker: Moran, Stahl & Boyer, Inc. press release, undated.

The Sixth Ordeal—The Tough Sell

99   Staying close to the customers: Thomas J. Peters and Robert H. Waterman, Jr., *In Search of Excellence* (New York: Harper & Row, 1982) This is Principle Two.

106   Westerman: Quoted from interview.

106   McKinsey Staff Paper on the failure rates on acquisitions: Steve Coley, "Diversification Through Acquisition," McKinsey White Paper, undated.

The Ninth Ordeal—The Breakdown of Loyalty

139   *Business Week* survey: Bruce Nussbaum, Kathleen Failla, Christopher S. Eklund, Alex Beam, James R. Norman, and Kathleen Deveny, "The End of Corporate Loyalty?" August 4, 1986.

140 Heidrick and Struggles survey: "The Mobile Manager," Heidrick and Struggles, Inc., Chicago, 1985, very kindly supplied to me by the firm.

140 "Corporate objectives ahead of personal gain": Ibid., p. 13.

141 Golden parachutes: "Employment Contracts and 'Golden Parachutes' In Corporate America" (New York: Gilbert Dwyer & Company, 1986).

141 Wyman's severance money: Peter J. Boyer, "CBS Gave Wyman $4.3 Million," *The New York Times*, April 7, 1987.

142 Tin parachutes: Alison Leigh Cowan, "New Ploy: 'Tin Parachutes'", *The New York Times*, March 19, 1987.

143 Severance deals for International Harvester and the Ford Motor Company: Ronald E. Berenbeim, "Company Programs to Ease the Impact of Shutdowns," A Research Report from the Conference Board, New York, 1986, pp. 25-53.

143 Silicon Valley data: Judith K. Larsen and Carolynn Mattison, "High Tech Lay-Offs: Silicon Valley and Silicon Glen," (Los Altos, CA: Cognos Associates, 1986).

144 Carl Icahn: "Confessions of a Corporate Raider," *Newsweek*, October 20, 1986, pp. 51-54.

148 Rosabeth Moss Kanter: Jenne Dorin McDowell, "Job Loyalty: Not the Virtue It Seems," *The New York Times*, March 3, 1985.

148 John Teets: Ibid.

148 Average job tenure figures: Albert R. Karr, *The Wall Street Journal*, May 19, 1987, p. 1.

148 Fred Hoag: Carol Hymowitz, "Stable Cycles of Executive Careers Shattered by Upheaval in Business," *The Wall Street Journal*, May 26, 1987.

149 Allegis corporation: Andrew Feinberg, "Changing the Name and Losing the Company," *The New York Times*, June 14, 1987.

149 Tom Peters: Tom Peters, "There Are No Excellent Companies," Tom Peters, *Fortune*, April 27, 1987.

150 Leveraged buyouts: Leslie Wayne, "'Reverse LBO's' Bring Riches," *The New York Times,* April 23, 1987.

150 Norman Macrae: Norman Macrae, "The Coming Entrepreneurial Revolution: A Survey," *The Economist,* December 25, 1976.

151 The two-tier setup: Amanda Bennett, "As Big Firms Continue to Trim Their Staffs, 2-Tier Setup Emerges," *The Wall Street Journal,* May 4, 1987.

152 Heidrick and Struggles survey: "The Mobile Manager," Heidrick and Struggles, Inc., Chicago, 1985.

The Tenth Ordeal—The Door

159 Federal Trade Commission: "Job-Hunting: Should You Pay?," *Facts for Consumers from the Federal Trade Commission,* fact sheet, Washington, D.C., October 1983.

161 David L. Birch: David L. Birch, "The Atomization of America," *INC.,* March 1987.

162 William C. Houze: William C. Houze, "Before the Resume," pamphlet, Association of Executive Search Consultants, Inc.

INDEX

A

A.T. Kearney, Inc., 151
Accountability, lack of, as signal, 131–132
Accountants, 52
  Big Eight, 52
  as source of information, 20–21
  employment security of, 84–85
ACME, 166–167
Acquired companies, deteriorating performance of, after acquisition, 65
Acquiring company, adopting the look of, 109
Acquisitions. *See also* Takeovers
  people with prior knowledge of, 19
Advanced Micro Devices, 17
Advertising, turnover of executives in, 148–149
Age, and your chances of being laid off, 82

Age discrimination, 136, 158
Age Discrimination in Employment Act, 156
Akers, John, 25
Allegis Corporation, 149
Allen, Paul, 52–53
AMF Inc., 14
Anderson, Howard, 25
Arrogance, of managers in acquiring company, 50
Artise, John, 20, 37–38, 153
Asset strippers, 43, 128
Association of Consulting Management Engineers. *See* ACME
Association of Executive Search Consultants, 145
Attitude
  importance of, in selling yourself to new owners, 106–107
  and successful survival of takeover, 89–92

Axline, Larry, 131

B

Backstabbing, 12, 111–122
  appearance of, vs. reality, 112
  counteracting your opponent in, 121–122
  and indispensability, 119–120
Barada, Paul W., 38
Barrett, James E., 85, 161
Behrendt, Bert, 168
Birch, David L., 161
Black, G. Arthur, 136
Blank, Diane Serafin, 159
Blue-collar workers, displacement by mergers, 3–4
Boesky, Ivan, 18, 22
Boss
  mysterious behavior of, as signal, 130
  nice, turned nasty, 133
  relationship with, as signal, 133
Boyer, Peter J., 23
Brady, Joseph J., 166–167
Buffett, Warren, 44
Bureau of Labor Statistics, survey of displaced managers and executives, 3–4
Burlington Industries, 21
Burton, John C., 53
Bushell, Jay, 82, 136, 147, 152
Business Week
  on success of mergers, 7
  survey of loyalty among management, 139–140
Busywork, during takeover, 77–78
Buyouts. *See also* Leveraged buyouts
  people with prior knowledge of, 19

C

Cardiff Acquisitions/Conwed Corporation, 14
Carrar, Annette, 160–161
CBS, 25
CBS News, 22–24, 26, 28, 139
CEOs
  displacement by mergers, 3
  getting to, to sell yourself, 106
Chajet, Clive, 149
Cleaning people, gossip from, value of, 20
Clients, relations with, during takeover's integration phase, 79
Coley, Steve, 64–67
Community service, assignment to, as signal, 132–133
Computers, replacement of people, 147
Computer search, on your new bosses, 36
Conference Board, survey of business shutdowns, 143
Consolidation committee, importance of membership on, 87
Consultants
  as hatchet men, 127
  relations with, information to be gained from, 126–127
Consultants News, 165
Consulting, 162–169
  growth of, 166–167
  professional organization for, 165
Consulting News, 170
Continental Can Company, 7
Continental Group, 16, 44, 61, 69
Continental International/Peter Kiewit Sons, 3, 7
Corky and Orky, 9–10
The Corporate Communications Report, 21
Corporate culture, 49–50, 55–56
Corporate debt, and hostile takeover fights, 9, 55
Cost-driven businesses, 55
Cuhney, Adam, 16

Index

Customers
  as aids in selling yourself to new owners, 108–109
  relations with, during takeover's integration phase, 79, 99–102

D

Davidson, Jeffrey P., 86
Deal makers, vs. operating managers, 43
Deals
  speed of closing, information revealed by, 43–45
  unresolved ambiguities in, information revealed by, 45–47
Demotion, significance of, 29
Denial
  definition of, 123
  overcoming, 12, 123–125
Depression, fighting off, during takeover, 73
Detrimental reliance, 157
Dingell, John, 2
Directory of Management Consultants, 165–166
Directory of Outplacement Firms, 159
Divestitures, 2
  proponents' arguments for, 5
Drake, Beam and Morin, 14
Dress, importance of, 109
DuPont/Conoco, 65
Dwyer, Gilbert E., 141–142

E

Economics, and your chances of being laid off, 82
Edelman, Asher, 21, 30–31, 142
Edgar, James M., 72, 91
Ellert, Wanda L., 39–40
Erhard, Werner, 75
est, 74–75
Executives. *See also* Managers
  displaced by mergers, 3
Executive search firms. *See* Headhunters
Expense reports, denial of, as signal, 128–129

F

Farley, Leon, 36–37
Fast-trackers, 52
Faunce, Stephen, 78
Federal Fair Credit Reporting Act, 39
Finance/accounting, management's emphasis on, 54
Financial engineering, 66
Firings, resulting from takeovers, 115
Fitting in, during takeover, 11, 81–97
Flexibility, importance of, during takeover, 89–93
Flexi-Van Corporation, 21
Flour Corporation/St. Joe Minerals Corporation, 7, 15
Ford Motor Company, 143
Fortune
  data on success of takeovers, 7
  survey of displacees, 4
Forty Plus, 93, 103–104, 160–161, 170
Free agent manager, 154
Frigeri, Arnold J., 58–59

G

Gallagher, Bob, 152
Gallagher, James J., 49
Gladhanding, 126
GM, 70
Going by the book, as means of backstabbing, 118
Golden parachutes, 141–142
Gossip, during takeovers, value of, 17–21
Gould, Bill, 146
Grapevines
  making use of, 17
  reliability of information from, 25–26

Grief, and combatting emotional
    paralysis, 73
Gulf + Western/Prentice Hall, 60

H

Hackworth, Donald E., 70
Half, Robert, 39, 109–110
Harcourt Brace Jovanovich, 10
Hartshorne, John F., 163, 165
Hatchet men
    consultants as, 127
    fate of, 134–135
Hazell, Robin T., 112
Headhunters
    contacting, for information on
        your new bosses, 38
    effect on loyalty, 144–146
    and privacy laws, 39–40
    treatment of fired vs.
        employed, 124
Heidrick and Struggles, Inc., survey on corporate loyalty,
    140, 152
Hendricks, Edward D., 167
Hip-pocket memos, 32–33
Hirsch, John, 154
Hoag, Fred, 148
Honesty. *See* Lies
Hostile takeovers, 2
    arguments against, 6
    threat of, effect on management performance, 8–9
    tin parachutes in, 142
Houze, William C., 162
Humphrey, David D., 168–169
Hunting band, 150–151

I

IBM, 24, 148
IBM/Rolm Corporation, 24–26
Icahn, Carl, 13
IMC. *See* Institute of Management Consultants
Indifference, as signal, 131–132
Indispensability
    and employment security,
        84–87

Indispensability *(Cont'd.)*
    from knowing where bodies are
        buried, dangers of,
        118–120
    managers who use subterfuge
        in gaining, 117–118
    and playing politics, 87–88
    psychological, 86–87
Information, importance of, during takeover's integration
    phase, 76–77
Information hotlines, in countering rumors, 33
Innovation-driven businesses, 55
Insider trading, 18–19
Institute of Management Consultants, 163, 165, 170
International Harvester, 143
Investment bankers, 44–45
Involvement, importance of, during takeover's integration
    phase, 77

J

Jacobs, Irwin, 14
Jemison, David, 42–44, 46
Job candidate, rationale, importance of, 162
Job(s)
    getting another, 159–162
    held by managers who have
        been displaced, 4
    numbers lost during mergers,
        14
Jovanovich, Peter, 10

K

Kanter, Rosabeth Moss, 148
Kennan, Mary, 60
Kennecott/Carborundum, 65
Kennedy, James H., 165, 167, 169
Korn/Ferry International, survey
    of senior managers' career
    backgrounds, 54, 58
Krist, Peter, 127, 128
Kroeger, Lin, 169
Kucera, Kathleen, 15–16

L

Lamalie Associates, survey of displaced executives, 3
Lawsuits, pros and cons, 136, 155–159
Lawyer
   help of, in severance negotiations, 158
   pros and cons of using, 12, 170
Layoffs, notice of, 17–18
Leadership, importance of, during takeover's integration phase, 77–78
Lee, Robert, 13
Legislation, and takeovers, 2
Leucardia National Corporation, 14
Leveling, 126
Leveraged buyouts, 2, 150
Levinson, Fredrica, 163–164
Levitt, Mitchell, 123–125
Lies
   avoiding, during takeover's integration phase, 76
   and money, 29
   official, 21–26
   during retention interview, 105
Lind, Douglass T., 71–73, 84, 120, 121
Liquidations, proponents' arguments for, 5
Loew's Hotels, 26–27
Log rolling, 115
Loyalty, 12
   breakdown of, 139–154
   decline in, 139–140
   definitions of, subscribed to by managers, 140
   faking, 152–154
   forces destroying, 144
   among laid-off workers, 143–144
   personal, 149–151, 154
   short-term, 154
   transferring, 149–151
   value of, 147–149

Luck questions, 81–83

M

MacDonald, Richard J., 28
Macrae, Norman, 150
Management Assistance Inc., 30, 142–143
Management teams, 160–161
Managers
   in acquired company, feelings of powerlessness, 59–64
   adaptation to takeover, 56
   displacement by mergers, numbers of, 3–4
   fired
      perceptions of, 124
      rationale for, 162
   terms of service, 148
   who quit, vs. managers who are fired, 51
Manne, Henry G., 5
Marineland, California, 9–10
Marriage ceremonies, information to be gleaned from, 40–41
MBAs, mobility of, 146–147
Meetings
   exclusion from, as signal, 133
   with your new bosses, information to be gleaned from, 40–42
Memo distribution, exclusion from, as signal, 133–134
Mentor, losing yours, 120, 131–132
Mergers. *See also* Partnership mergers; Takeovers
   activity, in 1987, 2
   effect on local communities, 9
   failures, 64–65
   opponents and proponents, arguments of, 5–10
   opportunity costs of, 9
   reasons for, 6
   taking a favorable position regarding, 106–107

Middle management, acquirer's attitude toward, and your chances of being laid off, 82–83
Miller, Bill, 28
Minorities
  firing of, during takeovers, 159
  opportunities for, in management, 58
Minstar/AMF Inc., 14
Mirvis, Philip, 55, 60
Mobil, 142
Mobil/Marcor, 7
Money, lies told by, 29
Monsanto, 7
Montgomery, Robert, 38–39, 145–147
Moran, Brian A., 31–33, 94
Motel 6, 151
Motivational training, 74
Murdoch, David, 21

N

Naj, Amal Kumar, 70
Name changes, corporate, effect on loyalty, 149
Naughton, Ward, 79, 99–100, 102, 103
Negotiation team, make-up of, information revealed by, 44
Networks
  and getting a new job, 104, 159
  informal, 101
  making use of, 18
  outside-company, 33–34
  using, to get information about new bosses, 41–42
  within-company, 19–20
New bosses
  as decent people, 57
  direct questioning of, 37
  knowledge of your business, 42–47
  researching, 11, 28, 35–47
New businesses, growth of, 161
North, Sid, 104–106

Number crunchers, prevalence of, in management, 54
Nymark, Richard, 167

O

Office, relocation, as signal, 134
Olney, Peter B., 126
Olsen, Frank A., 149
Operations people, employment security of, 85
Opportunity questions, 81, 83–89
Ordeals, 10
Oshman, Ken, 25
Outplacement, 12, 124, 159, 170
Outplacement consultants, 14, 18
Outten, Wayne N., 156

P

Pantry Pride/Revlon, 9
Pappas, Ike, 23, 24
Paranoia
  counteracting, 114–115
  dangers of, 113–114
Partnership mergers, 53
Passive resistance, among acquired company's workers, 75–76
Patience, and successful survival of takeover, 91
Pay, drop in, for displaced managers, 4
Peat Marwick/KMG Main Hurdman, 52–53
Performance appraisal, postponement of, as signal, 130–131
Perks, withdrawal of, as signal, 129–130
Personnel interviewers, approach to retention interviewing, 104–105
Peters, Tom, 75, 149
Phillip Morris/7-Up, 65
Phillips Petroleum, 7, 13
Pickens, T. Boone, 6, 7, 13
Plaintiff Employment Lawyers Association, 156–157, 170
Poison umbrella, 113

Index

Politics, and indispensability, 87–89
Post-acquisition value adding levers, 65–66
Powerlessness, feelings of, among managers of acquired company, 59–64
Pritchett, Price, 17, 25, 76–77
Private detective, hiring, to research your new bosses, 39
Privileges, withdrawal of, as signal, 129–130
Profitability, and mergers, 8
Proxmire, William, 2
Publishing, 56
  emphasis on finance/accounting in, 54–55

Q

Quaker/Stokely Van Camp, 66–67
Questions, asked of you by top management from acquiring company, 81–89
Quinn, Elizabeth, 164–165

R

Raiffa, Howard, 45
Rather, Dan, 23–24
Reference checking, 38–39, 112
Rein, Cathy, 44
Religion, and opportunities in management, 58
Relocating, 31, 93–96
Resentment
  of acquirers, among acquirees, 11, 50–67
  of golden parachutes, 141
  psychology of, 58–59
Retention interview, 11, 12, 102–104
  phony, 135–137
The Rights of Employees, 156
Risk arbitrage, 18
Rizzo, Paul J., 24–25
Robbins, Bob, 148–149
Rohatyn, Felix, 44

Rooney, Andy, 24
Rostenkowski, Dan, 2
Rumors, 100
  after the deal, 26–28
  assessing, 27–28
  before the deal, 15–17
  control of, companies' methods for, 30–33
  surrounding takeovers, 11, 13–34

S

Sales, Amy, 50
Sales people, employment security of, 84
Sando, Ernest, 21–22
Scapegoating, among acquiring managers, 62–63
Scharges, Horace, 30–31, 33, 142–143
Scherer, F.M., 8
Schiller, Marvin, 166
Schlumberger/Fairchild, 65
Schmitt, Christopher, 16
Schwarzman, Stephen A., 19
Secrecy, need for, in dealing with working papers, 32
Security clearance, downgrading, as signal, 129
Selling yourself
  to new owners, 11, 99–110
  pointers for, 102–106, 109–110
  to the right person, 106–109
Senior managers, former, as source of information, 21
Service-driven businesses, 55
Severance deals, 142
  lawyers' help in, 158
Severance pay, as incentive for liquidation team, 31
Sex, and opportunities in management, 58
Sexual harassment, 159
Shaw, Irving, 162, 165–167
Sholl, Calvin K., 84, 132–133
Short change, 125–126

Sigler, Andrew C., 9, 13
Silas, C.J. "Pete," 13, 26
Silence
 as signal, 128
 top management's, during takeovers, 16
Silicon Valley, 16, 143
Singer, Adrianne C., 25
Sitkin, Sim, 42–44, 46
Slater, Pat, 93, 103–104
Sleeping bosses, 127–128
Small businesses
 employment opportunities in, 161, 170
 success of takeovers in, 57
Snyder.General Corporation/McQuay, Inc., 14
Society of Professional Management Consultants, 165
St. Joe Minerals Corporation, 15
Stay bonus, 127
Stock prices, effects of takeover on, 6–7, 18–19
Stress interview, 105–106
Stringer, Howard, 23, 27
Sturm, Donald L., 7
Subordinates, relations with, during takeover's integration phase, 76–79
Sullivan, John P., 19–20, 126
Systems people, employment security of, 84

T

Takeovers. See also Hostile takeovers; Mergers
 failures, 57
 integration phase
  do something vs. doing nothing during, 72–73
  gaining reputation as worker during, 71–72
 legislative efforts to curb, 2
 in new business areas, 57
 reasons for, 5–6
 seller-initiated, 65
 successful, 65–66

Takeovers (Cont'd.)
 targets of, characteristics, 101
Taylor, Frederick, 166
Teets, John, 148
Ten Eyck, Richard C., 73–74
Thomson S.A./Mostek, 16
Tin parachutes, 142
Tisch, Lawrence, 22–24, 26–28, 139, 141
Toastmasters, 104
Tobias, Paul H., 156–159, 170
Top management, reliability of information from, 25
Track record, and your chances of being laid off, 83–84
Trevor, Leigh B., 6, 8, 14
Troublemaking, in counteracting log rolling, 117
Trump, Donald, 149
Tucker, Michael, 96
Turner, Ted, 22
Turner Broadcasting System, 22
TWA, 144
Two-tier setup, 151

U

Unicol, 7
United Airlines, 149
U.S. Steel, 149
USX, 149

V

Visibility, importance of, during takeover's integration phase, 77

W

Wallace, Mike, 24
Wall Street, 15
Wall Street analysts, and rumor analysis, 28
Warren, Richard B., 113–114, 115, 117, 128–130
Waters, Tim, 10
Weber, David, 9
Wells Fargo/Crocker National Bank, 3

Westerman, Jewell, 106–107
Westin, Alan, 153
Wickes/Gamble-Skogmo, 7
Women
   firing of, during takeovers, 159
   opportunities for, in management, 58
Work, during takeover, 11, 69–79
Worker-bee approach, 70–72

Work-for-hire arrangements, 151
Wright, Joseph R., Jr., 5
Wyman, Thomas H., 141

X-Y-Z

Xerox/SDS, 65
Zemke, Ron, 74
Ziebarth, John, 160–161